PRAISE FOR *INVEST LIKE A COUCH POTATO*

Scott Burns has produced an engaging journey through the intricacies of investing for and during retirement. His advocacy of the Couch Potato investing style—using a small number of low-cost, well-diversified index funds—is a pragmatic and effective solution for any retiree. Savor this book's clear writing style and pithy wisdom.

—**William P. Bengen,** Author of *A Richer Retirement:*
Supercharging the 4% Rule to
Spend More and Enjoy More

For a third of a century, Scott Burns's Couch Potato Portfolio has provided his lucky readers with a smooth and effortless ride to easy street. If you missed it the first time around, or if you need a refresher, then you won't do better than *Invest Like a Couch Potato:* read, enjoy, and prosper.

—**William J. Bernstein,** bestselling author of
The Investor's Manifesto: Preparing for Prosperity,
Armageddon, and Everything in Between

Forget overwrought financial guidance. In *Invest Like a Couch Potato,* Scott Burns resists the urge to tell us everything he knows about investing (a lot!). Instead, he gives us something even more valuable: what we *need* to know about investing. I enjoyed every bit of this wise book.

—**Christine Benz,** Director of Personal Finance and
Retirement Planning, Morningstar

Invest Like a Couch Potato packs enough wisdom, humility, clarity, and humor to be the best personal finance book of the decade!

—**Andrew Hallam,** international bestselling author of
Millionaire Teacher, Millionaire Expat, and *Balance*

Scott Burns is America's deeply beloved financial therapist. He's spent decades protecting millions of us from two terrible dangers—our impulses and Wall Street's con jobs. *Invest Like a Couch Potato* is classic Burns—a brilliant, less-is-more, common-sense path to financial well-being and peace of mind. It's a must read—for you and everyone you love.

> —**Laurence Kotlikoff,** Boston University professor of economics and *New York Times* bestselling personal finance author

A fun and essential guide to investments and, of even greater importance, life.

> —**John Rekenthaler**

A remarkably clear and insightful guide to money—and to securing the freedom to live life on your own terms. A brilliantly crafted and genuinely enjoyable read.

> —**Allan Roth,** financial planner, columnist, and author of *How a Second Grader Beat Wall Street*

With the insight of a seasoned columnist and the tone of a trusted friend, Scott Burns demonstrates how surprisingly little effort is required to invest well. His Couch Potato method has eased the worries of thousands, and it can help you feel more relaxed and confident about your future.

> —**Dan Solin,** author of the Smartest series of investing books

INVEST LIKE A COUCH POTATO

SCOTT BURNS

INVEST LIKE A COUCH POTATO

ACHIEVE FINANCIAL SECURITY AND LIFETIME FREEDOM WITH EASE

WILEY

For general information on our other products and services or for technical support, please contact our Customer Care Department within the United States at (800) 762-2974, outside the United States at (317) 572-3993 or fax (317) 572-4002.

Wiley also publishes its books in a variety of electronic formats. Some content that appears in print may not be available in electronic formats. For more information about Wiley products, visit our web site at www.wiley.com.

Library of Congress Cataloging-in-Publication Data is Available:

ISBN 9781394366866 (Cloth)
ISBN 9781394366880 (ePDF)
ISBN 9781394366873 (ePub)

Cover Design: Wiley
Cover Image: © wir0man/Getty Images
Author Photo: Courtesy of the Author

Printed by CPI Group (UK) Ltd, Croydon CR0 4YY

C9781394366866_090126

To Carolyn, my amazing, wonderful, and loving wife.

CONTENTS

CONTENTS

CONTENTS

INTRODUCTION: AN EASY STROLL TO INVESTMENT SUCCESS AND A BETTER LIFE

The more relaxed you are, the better you are at everything: the better you are with your loved ones, the better you are with your enemies, the better you are at your job, the better you are with yourself.

—Bill Murray

This book will guide you to a rich and fulfilling life.

It begins with facing a primary life task, saving and investing enough while we are working to sustain us during the many years we are not working.

It ends with demonstrations of how much you will benefit from absolute simplicity. The benefit is measured in financial wealth. It is also measured in the other kinds of wealth that you will gain, wealth that would otherwise be lost in our obsessive money culture.

More than 30 years ago I introduced readers of my syndicated personal finance column to Couch Potato investing. If you can fog a mirror and divide by the number 2 (if necessary, with the aid of a handheld calculator), you can manage your investments.

Seriously.

Simply invest in a low-cost index fund of domestic stocks and a low-cost index fund of domestic bonds and you can accumulate the financial wealth needed to fund a healthy retirement. Better still, you will probably enjoy a better return than at least 80 percent of the people who spend more time and pay more in fees.

Think about that.

Is it sane to choose a 20 percent chance of investment success over an 80 percent chance?

DOES COUCH POTATO INVESTING WORK?

You bet. One of the reasons that I continue to write is the immense satisfaction I get from reader letters thanking me for helping them find their way to a generously funded retirement. Some readers write to tell me they have put together collections of columns to give to their sons and daughters.

In addition, I will show you the proof of the pudding. That's a regular report I do that shows how much principal is left after withdrawing an inflation-adjusted sum each year from savings. It's important to note this report doesn't list percentages or rates of return. It lists actual money remaining after periods of 3, 5, 10, 15, 20, 25, 30, and 35 years.

It's all about the actual money.

The results routinely show that you can pay virtually no attention to investing and still pay your bills in retirement. That means you can devote your time and energy to everything else in your life:

- The work you love
- The people you love
- The projects that provoke your passion

That's more than the proverbial win-win. It's a win-win-win-win.

THE MANAGED ALTERNATIVES DON'T WORK

Now compare Couch Potato Investing to all the confusing, expensive, and time-consuming alternatives.

Your local bookstore is filled with books that tell you how to build financial wealth and become "rich." Some of those books are quite lengthy. Most are complicated. Some are long *and* complicated. I've seen a few that should be sold by the pound.

Virtually all these books require that you be interested in the subject. They demand that you acquire a huge working knowledge.

How huge? Well, it's a long list.

Here are just a few of the words most people know little or nothing about: stocks, bonds, cash, money market funds, open and closed end mutual funds, exchange traded funds, certificates of deposit, savings accounts, Treasury securities, stock options, real estate investment trusts, cash value life insurance, annuities, optimization, variance, standard deviation. The list goes on.

And on.

The Investopedia website has 13,000 definitions. The *Oxford Dictionary of Finance and Banking* includes over 5,500 definitions. And that's just to start!

None of this knowledge is required to be a successful investor. Indeed, it could be said that the more knowledge you acquire, the greater the odds that you will make bad decisions. Those bad decisions are likely to fill you with regret, remorse, self-recriminations, and anger.

Choosing the Couch Potato Way, once you understand that it works, should be a no-brainer. Literally.

Unfortunately, it isn't.

Every day all of us are subject to a fire hose of media content suggesting that we will benefit from investing in this, that, or some other thing. It is virtually inescapable. It shows up on our phones, our visits to news providers, our watching of daily television, our magazines and our newspapers.

Whatever the source, the content insists that acting *today* is important and that someone knows something that you don't. In fact, *no one* knows the future. The only certainty in all that information is that everyone involved is making a living from it.

At your expense.

Finally, there is another reason this book is short.

In addition to respecting *your* time, I treasure mine. I am 84 years old, way too old to squander what remains of the precious gift we receive at birth.

If you want to know exactly how to become a Couch Potato investor right now, just skip to Part III, How to Invest Your Savings. It will tell you what funds to buy. It will show you the bonus of low-cost compound growth while you are saving and accumulating. It will also show you the bonus of low-cost compound growth while you are dis-saving and spending your nest egg.

That, by the way, is a big deal.

Just fold down the corner of the page and start reading. From there you can skip to Part VII, More Couch Potato Cookbook – Exactly How to Do It. It will tell you what to do for each of the major investing platforms. It will also suggest some options that may be available in your employer's 401(k) or 403(b) plan. And if you are a federal employee, it will tell you how to use the Thrift Savings Plan and why you should avoid the annuity salespeople who will besiege you at retirement.

But I don't expect you to take anything on faith.

WHAT HUMANS ACTUALLY DO

In Part I, The Human Life Cycle, you'll read about the human life cycle and how it puts all of us in the same mortal boat. You'll see what it looks like in actual cash spending and how it effects – in a very nice way – how much you need to save.

Spoiler alert: Less.

It will also show you the sublime benefit of death.

A TOUR OF THE INVESTMENT BATTLEFIELD

In Part II, The Long, Glorious History of Investment Failure, you'll be introduced to the facts of what you've probably already experienced: the media mythology storm that tells us, minute by minute, why we need to buy or sell *now* and how this or that will make us rich. Fortunately, we've got Weston Wellington to show us how untrue every claim is. No one knows the future, no matter how much they demand in payment.

HOW TO INVEST YOUR SAVINGS

If you like to take things on faith and want to start investing right now, just skip to Part III, How to Invest Your Savings. That's where you'll learn about the least expensive exchange-traded funds and how to buy them almost anywhere. You'll also learn that return on investment notions that aren't the most basic can sometimes be higher, but not when you adjust for risk.

You'll learn about the benefits of low-cost index investing while accumulating and, later, while spending in retirement – measured in actual spending power. Finally, I provide the answer to a question everyone asks: "How can I spend more?"

REASSURANCE, IN DOLLARS

In Part IV, The Proof Is in the Pudding, you'll see exactly how much cash retirees have had left if they take the Couch Potato Investing path. I've called this the *Pudding Report* because that's where the proof is. You'll see how much principal is left for periods of 3, 5, 10, 15, 20, 25, 30, and 35 years based on withdrawing 4 or 5 percent of your nest egg in the first year and then increasing that dollar amount by the rate of inflation each year from age 65 to age 100.

That withdrawal rate is based on the work of William Bengen, the financial planner who shocked the advisory world by introducing the reality of investment ups and downs. You'll also learn how much wiggle room you have for taking more without increasing the risk of too much month at the end of the money.

MEASURING THE BENEFITS OF COUCH POTATO INVESTING

In Part V, The Rewards of Simplicity for Actual People, you'll learn how "average" gets a bad rap. You'll be reminded of why "perfect is the enemy of good." You'll also be introduced to all the benefits of simplicity that are ignored by the money-is-all people. You'll learn that there are five kinds of wealth – not one – and that wealth addiction is a problem.

The time and energy you save are your tools to avoid being a techno-serf in the economy coming toward us.

THE HIDDEN VALUES IN OUR UN-MONEY ECONOMY

In Part VI, The Rewards Found Elsewhere, you'll learn about the low-hanging fruit outside of investing – like home ownership for some, the beneficial feedback loop of saving, and the fruit of that feedback loop in the financial independence/retire early (FIRE) option.

COOKING THE COUCH POTATO WAY

Part VII, More Couch Potato Cookbook – Exactly How to Do It, expands what you learned in Part III, exploring the specifics of Couch Potato Investing choices. It also introduces how you might invest if you feel, as many do, that the entire world is going through a major change that requires rethinking how much you invest in the United States.

A BIBLIOGRAPHY YOU CAN READ

In Part VIII, The Data That Supports Everything I've Said, you'll take a stroll through the books and research papers that have been the foundation of Couch Potato Investing, just so you know why if you want to learn more.

The really good news here is that simplicity is a virtue, so just dive in.

CHAPTER ONE

WHAT HAPPENS WHEN AN ASPIRING ASTRONAUT AND BIOLOGIST BECOMES A WRITER

Man plans, God laughs.

—Yiddish proverb

did not intend to become a writer. At 16 I had a plan. I was going to be an astronaut. I was going to the moon.

Maybe further.

First, I learned how to fly, which I did using money I made mowing lawns. This was 1957, the year Russia launched the first earth satellite, *Sputnik*.

It weighed 193.8 pounds. The United States launched our first at the end of January 1958. It weighed a dainty 30.66 pounds.

To be an astronaut I had to be an engineer. I would also need to go to the Massachusetts Institute of Technology (MIT) because, well, the first astronauts would be from a place like MIT.

How did I know this? Easy. I had read an Arthur C. Clarke short story, "Superiority". It was about an intergalactic war in which one side lost its technological lead and, therefore, the war.

A blurb on a paperback told me it was required reading at MIT.

In spring 1958, my senior year at Princeton High School, I was looking for a way to explore oxygen production by Chlorella algae. I figured it would be necessary for longer term stays on the moon. So I went to Guyot Hall. I met Professor Gerhard Fankhauser on the staircase. He was chairman of the Princeton University biology department. He adopted me and gave me a part-time job taking care of his salamanders (and his two treasured haploid axolotls).

I never learned about oxygen production.

But I developed an interest in the math of growth and form, statistics, distribution patterns, and life cycles. I also learned that the British Thermal Unit, not the dollar, is the fundamental currency of all life. The money we humans create is a sloppy shadow on the wall of Plato's cave.

And, yes, I went to MIT, an event that surprised many, including my high school guidance counselor.

ADVANCED DILETTANTE STUDIES

But I did not become an engineer. I discovered that I liked writing more, that I *needed* to write. Like most life changes, it was a passionate discovery, not a choice. And MIT, being the amazing, flexible institution it is, let me organize a creative writing course, perhaps the first, not to mention take courses up the river at rival Harvard.

As someone with a degree in what might be called Advanced Dilettante Studies, finding employment wasn't a slam dunk. But, in addition to books, I've been writing columns for more than 50 years. First for glossy magazines. Then for newspapers. I have loved writing a newspaper column, particularly for my many years at the *Dallas Morning News*.

I tell you all this for a reason.

BELIEF SAYS SMARTS COUNT; THE DATA SAYS OTHERWISE

My education made it very difficult to give up the idea that smart people could make superior investment decisions. But as the data sources, software, and personal computers developed, it became inescapably clear that paying up for investment results was absolute folly.

Year after year the data revealed that low costs were important, that good stories about investment managers were just that: good stories. Good long-term results were not included.

The biggest contributor to this knowledge for actual people, not institutions, has been Morningstar. Formed in 1984, Morningstar introduced mutual fund screening software and started reporting on mutual funds with the individual investor in mind. If you're not familiar with Morningstar I urge you to visit their website and explore.

Providing tools to individual investors is important because it meant being able to do research on a widely available and inexpensive tool. People could duplicate results for themselves, one of the big tests of research. It was power to the people, not pronouncements from institutions with a vested interest.

By 1991, I felt there was enough data to demonstrate that a dirt simple index fund portfolio would do well enough that a person with absolutely no interest in stocks, bonds, or investing could rise from total sloth for a few minutes a year and achieve results that were better than most. I introduced the first Couch Potato portfolio.

Note that it wasn't the "best" portfolio. Or the "perfect" portfolio. Perfect is the enemy of good. It's the portfolio that will let you focus on all that things that are truly important. They have little to do with money and investing.

GOING STOCHASTIC

Three years later, famed investment advisor William Bengen added the word *stochastic* to the vocabulary of reluctant financial planners. I was at the financial planners annual meeting in San Diego when he spoke and presented the research he had done on safe withdrawal rates. It was mind-blowing.

Prior to that, financial planners had been happy to use the simple compounding methods that routinely showed magnificent results – without reflecting the impact of market risk.

Why did simple compounding show magnificent results? It ignored the regular and significant ups and downs of asset prices. Bengen included the reality of fluctuating market prices. He found that a basic retirement portfolio could have a base withdrawal rate of 4 to 4.5 percent and survive through a long retirement.

One year later, a much larger legend made a contrary assertion. Peter Lynch declared, in *Worth* magazine, that you could have an all-stock retirement portfolio and reliably withdraw 7 percent a year. Lynch was the mastermind of Fidelity Magellan fund.

Lynch was dead wrong. He was shocked when I told him.

I disproved his assertion by sitting down with Ken Bingham, a broker friend. We used software and data from the American Funds Group that wasn't available to the public.

If you followed Peter Lynch, you had a 50 percent chance of being flat broke at an awkward age.

Fidelity was, and remains, an amazing brain trust. But it took years before they incorporated Bengen's stochastic reality into the information they offered the public. "Fido," in my opinion, is one of the better institutions that handle our money. Truth and honesty are further away at most.

That's why we need to take information we receive from the marketing departments of our investing institutions with a full measure of salt. We need to do the same with much that passes for investment research.

Why? Statistical work is easily manipulated.

Yes, that's depressing.

But while the marketing side of investing leads us to a Tower of Babel, lies, and ever-increasing complexity, we have a positive alternative. If we start with the very basics of human life, we'll find simplicity and truth. They, in turn, can lead us to financial independence and personal freedom.

We are all unique. But what we share, as creatures, is more powerful.

RELATED COLUMNS

Scott Burns, "The Importance of Being a Dull Investor," 9/29/1991, https://scottburns
.com/on-the-importance-of-being-a-dull-investor/

Scott Burns, "Dangerous Advice from Peter Lynch," 10/1/1995, https://scottburns
.com/dangerous-advice-from-peter-lynch/

Scott Burns, "The New Skepticism," 2/22/2015, https://scottburns.com/the-
new-skepticism/

Scott Burns, "Count Your Fathers," 6/1/2015, https://scottburns.com/count-
your-fathers/

SOURCES AND REFERENCES

Arthur C. Clarke, "Superiority," https://www.baen.com/Chapters/1439133476/
1439133476___5.htm

Wikipedia for Peter Lynch, https://en.wikipedia.org/wiki/Peter_Lynch

Wikipedia for Professor Gerhard Fankhauser, https://en.wikipedia.org/wiki/
Gerhard_Fankhauser

Wikipedia for William Bengen, https://en.wikipedia.org/wiki/William_Bengen

PART I

THE HUMAN LIFE CYCLE: WE SHARE MORE THAN YOU THINK

CHAPTER TWO

WHAT SEVEN BILLION HUMANS WANT

This did not annoy Amanda for she had long believed that humans were invented by water, as a device for transporting itself from one place to another.
—Tom Robbins, *Another Roadside Attraction*

Life for we humans is exquisitely complicated and unendingly varied. We are all quite different.

If you are reading this book, it's a good bet you know this. The odd thing is that we act surprised!

We raise our eyebrows. We give others quizzical looks, as though our lack of uniformity was astounding.

I have no explanation for this.

It makes me think about the nature of water.

If each crystal snowflake in a snowstorm is unique, although entirely composed of one molecule – pure water – wouldn't it be weird if human beings, who are composed of 30 trillion cells, each filled with more than a thousand long chains of complicated carbon compounds, exhibited any uniformity at all?

So, yeah, we're all different. Exquisitely, mysteriously, different.

Even reducing our lives to a matter of finance, of getting and spending money, is unendingly different because each of us is a tweak or shade different here and there. Or somewhere else.

But don't throw up your hands. Enjoy a moment of anarchic ecstasy instead.

THE BIG SAMENESS

Now join me to explore the sublime comfort of our big sameness.

We are born, we grow, we learn, we earn our keep, we mate, we procreate, we age, we weaken, we die. A few of these actions are more difficult than others. Somewhere in all that we hope to love and be loved. We seek to do something worthwhile. We hope to build a future. And we'd like to avoid hunger, cold, and discomfort.

Skeptics should consider the efforts we make to marry and live happily ever after. Some people do this again and again, despite the famed quote from Samuel Johnson that "a second marriage is a triumph of hope over experience."

I can speak personally to this. When Carolyn and I married in 1995 I was 54 years old and divorced. Older but still hopeful, we married in the Chapel at Loretto in Santa Fe, New Mexico, an intimate space famed for its "miraculous stair" – an all-wood spiral staircase of mysterious origin. She still smiles when I refer to her as my "permanent wife."

Most people give up on the institution at three or more marriages. That explains why the Census Bureau stops counting at three. Still, we've always got the example of the late Mickey Rooney. He married eight times. (I've always thought he should have stopped at Ava Gardner, but maybe he didn't have a choice.)

Indefatigable hope!

OUR MATING HABITS, UP CLOSE AND PERSONAL

A romantic study by the Census Bureau titled "Number, Timing, and Duration of Marriages and Divorces" is regularly updated. It can tell us a lot about our collective efforts to find love, peace, and security. Reporting on the state of marriage in 1996, for instance, the study found that 96.6 percent of women were unmarried at age 15–19 (mostly likely good news, that) but the percentage declined dramatically, reaching a mere 4.2 percent for women 70 and over.

Think about that. A stunning 95.8 percent of women eventually married in 1996.

The percentage of women married once and still married peaked at 57 percent between ages 30 and 34. It fell dramatically for age 70 and over. But divorce wasn't the cause. They were widowed.

The most recent update of the study, reporting on 2016, showed an increase in the percentage of women who never married in younger ages, but by age 70 or older only 4.9 percent of all women had never married.

So, for all the hype about the end of marriage, most women still marry at sometime during their lives. Ditto, men. By age 70 or older only 4.9 percent have never married.

Dividing our population by race and applying the same measurements shows that there are differences in our mating habits. But in terms of direction, we're all the same.

(Note to men who are not married: If you want to maximize your chance of a marriage that lasts, the figures suggest that a cautious man will marry an Asian woman with a college education and a good income. More than 90 percent of these women marry only once. In the other direction, Asian men are most likely to be married only once.)

Screening by race alone, the probability declines to 83 percent for Hispanic and Pacific Islander women and about 75 percent for white and Black women.

THE MARRIAGE DREAM DEFERRED

Another message in the statistics is that marriage, for everyone, is being deferred. In the 1960s, for instance, it was common for women to marry shortly after graduation. Indeed, a girl at a Boston finishing school once told me that her school motto was "a ring by spring or double your money back." In 1970, the median age at first marriage for women was 20.8 years. For men it was 23.2 years.

But that was then.

By 2016, the median age at first marriage was 28 for women and 30 for men. That's a huge shift in less than half a century.

It's also a huge shift in another thing that affects our long-term financial lives: the birth rate. With the median age at first marriage for women rising by over seven years, our entire society has lost seven years of prime child bearing time. The impact has been demographically catastrophic. Our national birth rate has fallen from its peak of 3.7 children per woman in 1957 to 1.66 births per woman in 2022.

Provisional data for 2023, the last data collected as I write this, shows the birth rate continues to decline, having reached 1.62 births per woman.

SLIPPING PROCREATION

This has not happened because Americans have lost interest in procreation. Indeed, for a few years demographers carefully noted that some of the decline in childbearing at young ages had simply shifted to women 30 and over.

But that's the rub. Those lost years can't be replaced. It is difficult, if not impossible, to fully compensate by having more children later in life.

Nor is the falling birth rate the result of our not wanting to have children. Survey after survey has shown that American women, on average, would like to have 2.5 children. That's more than the 2.1 births per woman required for a stable population. It's also vastly more than the 0.76 birth rate for South Korea, the country most likely to disappear over the next hundred years.

THE LIFE CYCLE PREVAILS

But in the United States of America, we want to marry, have children, and nurture them. That means all of us, including those, male or female, who prefer same-sex relationships. It's our big sameness.

It is something to be celebrated.

As you will see in coming chapters, the big sameness is a benefit, not a liability, for lifetime financial sustenance. It's something we should be thankful for because it will help us deal with the problems created by the worldwide decline in birthrates – an explosion of retirees looking for retirement benefits from a shrinking population of workers.

Another bit of good news is the flow of immigrants to the United States. It turns out that immigration will offset some of the decline in our birthrate. This isn't happening for Russia or China. Nor is it happening for South Korea or Japan. Those countries, not to mention all of Europe, will be struggling with the economic woes of depopulation.

That's why YouTube offers a multitude of regular videos of houses available, some for next to nothing, in Spain, Portugal, Italy, France, and Japan.

THE LITERAL FOUNDATION OF PERSONAL FINANCE

All of this is, literally, the foundation of personal finance. It determines the shape of our lives as workers and savers. It informs our retirement. And the money we use is just a series of shopping notes written along the way.

RELATED COLUMNS

Scott Burns, "Revisiting the Past to Learn About the Future," 11/9/2004, https://scottburns.com/revisiting-the-past-to-learn-about-the-future/

Scott Burns, "Trust Me, Your Retirement Will Be Longer Than David Bach Predicts," 10/12/2018, https://scottburns.com/trust-me-your-retirement-will-be-longer-than-david-bach-predicts/

Scott Burns, "Sandbagging the Pursuit of Happiness," 9/10/2022, https://scottburns.com/sandbagging-the-pursuit-of-happiness/

SOURCES AND REFERENCES

Current Population Reports, "Number, Timing, and Duration of Marriages and Divorces: 2016," https://www.census.gov/content/dam/Census/library/publications/2021/demo/p70-167.pdf

Institute for Family Studies, "How Many Kids Do Women Want?" 6/1/2018, https://ifstudies.org/blog/how-many-kids-do-women-want#:~:text=That%20personal%20ideal%20may%20still,%2C%20in%20others%2C%20it's%20lower

National Center for Health Statistics, "U.S. Fertility Rate Drops to Another Historic Low," 4/25/2024, https://www.cdc.gov/nchs/pressroom/nchs_press_releases/2024/20240525.htm

Salzburg Global, "South Korea's Fertility Rate Should Be a Warning to the World," 9/30/2024: https://ifstudies.org/blog/how-many-kids-do-women-want#:~:text=That%20personal%20ideal%20may%20still,%2C%20in%20others%2C%20it's%20lower

CHAPTER THREE

MEASURING THE BIG SAMENESS IN CASH: THE REVISED EQUIVALENCE SCALE

If you want to change the world go home and love your family.
—Mother Teresa

W e humans have a life cycle. We are born, nurtured, and educated. We seek a mate, we share expenses, we marry. We have a child, maybe two. Sometimes we have three. We nurture the child/children. We educate same.

After that we live as "empty nesters." We grow old. One spouse dies. The surviving spouse lives on, alone.

How we do this varies greatly. Whether we do it successfully also varies greatly. Some people have wonderful memories of loving, nurturing parents. Others invest their adult lives trying to build the family of origin they wish they had.

Some kids are raised poor and unnurtured and never overcome the original deficit.

Some kids are raised rich and overindulged. They live their lives handicapped by entitlement.

Parent or child, we're all different. We all have a story to tell. Curiously, it will be a very different story from the one our siblings (or parents) will tell.

But the basic structure of our path is the same.

The result is seen in three different measures. One, our life cycle, is fundamental. The other two are more procedural. One is lifetime saving and taxation. The other is lifetime debt service.

CLIMBING THE MONEY MOUNTAIN

Let's start with the life cycle stuff first.

My favorite tool for measuring the actual dollar cost of the American life cycle was created in 1968. It's called the *revised equivalence scale*, a page of index numbers that vary the cost of living by age, household size, and household composition. To be sure, it's not perfect.

But nothing is.

Another measure, the MIT Living Wage Index, is more contemporary. But it's also less complete because it only adjusts expenses by household size, not for age. The figures in that index, however, confirm the long arc of the revised equivalence scale.

If you arrange the index numbers along a chronological scale from being single at 18 to being married, having children and raising them to age 18, one gigantic factoid emerges.

There is no way to sugarcoat this.

Our decision to marry and have children is wildly heroic. Awesome, really.

Your cost of living is almost certain to rise faster than your household income for a simple reason. For most people, wage gains are small. But the cost of raising a child rises fast.

How fast? Try twice as fast as typical wage gains, sometimes more.

Worse, that isn't the scariest part. Whether we're talking about the revised equivalence scale, the regular measurement of child-rearing costs by the Department of Agriculture or the MIT Living Wage Index, costs beyond age 18 aren't considered.

A NOT SO MINOR OMISSION

So little things like sending a kid to college aren't considered. To be sure, some kids are told they're on their own at their 18th birthday or when they graduate from high school. Their doting parents wish them well, give them a ham sandwich, and push them out the door.

"Write if you get work," they say.

At the posh end of the scale, other kids get regular family vacations in the Caribbean even as full tuition is being paid to, say, Yale, Stanford, or Duke, and they arrive at school in a nifty new Tahoe SUV. At the University of Mississippi, it has been told, some of the young women have interior designers for their rooms.

Other kids get what might be called *the long ride*. In addition to a generous college education experience, their parent's foot the bill for all medical school expenses or things like combinations of an MBA degree and odd graduate degree disciplines like maritime or patent law.

Most of our kids are somewhere in between, but it's not difficult to imagine that the most recent Department of Agriculture cost for raising a child, a whopping $233,610 in 2017, is easily duplicated in four years at Harvard where the all-in (but cautious) annual cost was between $86,000 and $91,000 for the 2024–2025 school year. (That explains why I was so happy that three of our grandchildren went to Texas A&M, where the annual cost is now about $30,000.)

You can get an idea of how heroic the basic project of forming a family and deciding to have children is by looking at Figure 3.1. It's a steep climb.

Figure 3.1   The Life Cycle Mountain: Consumption Index Using the Revised Equivalence Scale

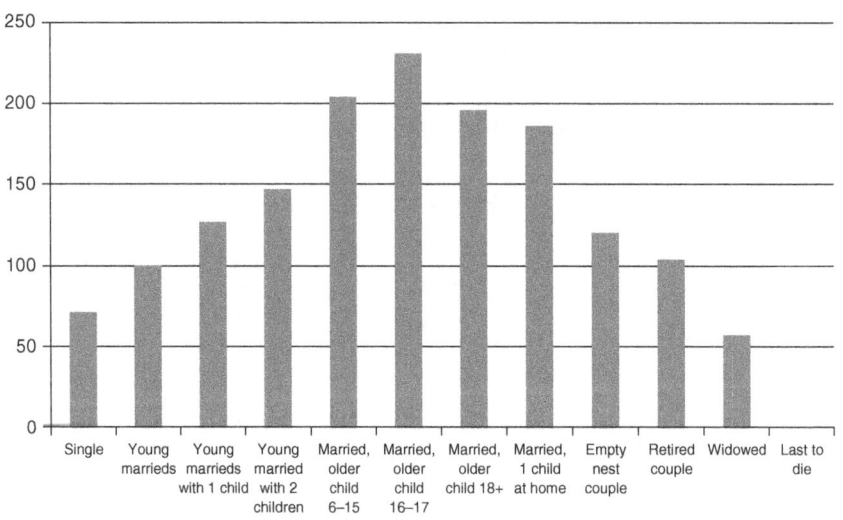

Table 3.1 Life Cycle Income Need.

Household Status	Years Married	Age	Consumption Index
Single	Na	24	71
Young marrieds	0	25	100
Young marrieds with 1 child	3	28	127
Young marrieds with 2 children	5	30	147
Married, older child 6–15	10	35	204
Married, older child 16–17	19	44	231
Married, older child 18+	21	46	196
Married, 1 child at home	25	50	186
Empty nest couple	30	55	120
Retired couple	40	65+	104
Widowed	Na	65+	57
Last to die			

Table 3.1 shows another way of seeing the same data.

I've set the cost of living for a young married couple at an index number of 100. By that index number, the cost of living for a single person is an index number of 71. So, if two people were living separately and were self-supporting, by sharing resources (mostly shelter) they would enjoy a significant economic benefit – their income would be 142 while their expenses would be 100, a 42 percent surplus.

Clearly, living together is a big plus.

But that all ends with the decision to have children. The cost-of-living index rises to 127 with the first child, 147 with the second, 204 when the first child is ages 6–15, and 231 when the older child is ages 16–17.

So, their real cost of living more than doubles in about 19 years. That calculates to a 4.5 percent real annual compound rate of increase. Adjust for the long-term inflation rate, a bit over 3 percent, and wages need to grow at about a 7.5 percent annually for nearly two decades.

Not too likely.

Average worker wage gains, however, have risen at a nominal rate of 3–5 percent in recent decades so most young parents have trouble maintaining their personal standard of living in the entire 19-year period from the birth of the first child to its 18th birthday.

Can anything counterbalance this?

Not really. A persnickety economist could say that young people enjoy relatively large raises early in their careers. True enough.

But the large gains fade after about eight years. Worse, my index figure sets marriage at age 25. That's early career. By marrying later, as the young are doing today, those big raises are fading in the rearview mirror by the time the first child is born.

I believe, and have maintained for decades, that this is good news. How could that be possible?

Easy. *We don't have to replace a standard of living that we never had!* And since most financial plans are based on replacing your gross income, not your standard of living as a couple, most financial plans are dead wrong. They urge you to save enough to replace income that you've never spent on yourself or your spouse.

Now look back at Figure 3.1. All those bars rising over the number 100 represent a standard of living you never had. It's income that was spent raising children.

It's a whole lot and it's not for a few years. It's for two decades, probably longer.

This is a big deal.

RELATED COLUMNS

Scott Burns, "Why Young Families Are Always Broke," 8/21/2005, https://scott burns.com/why-young-families-are-always-broke/

Scott Burns, "Why Divorce Will Lower Your Standard of Living," 9/3/2006, https:// scottburns.com/why-divorce-will-lower-your-standard-of-living/

Scott Burns, "Living on Social Security in Texas," 3/13/2023, https://scottburns.com/living-on-social-security-in-texas/

Scott Burns, "Hey, Take the Day Off," 7/5/1998, https://scottburns.com/hey-take-the-day-off/

Scott Burns, "Life of Riley Index, Retiree Version," 10/27/1998, https://scottburns.com/the-life-of-riley-index-retiree-version-2/

Scott Burns, "Future Retirees Will Pay More in Taxes," 4/10/2005, https://scottburns.com/future-retirees-will-pay-more-taxes/

Scott Burns, "Introducing the 94 Percent," 2/13/2004, https://scottburns.com/introducing-the-94-percent/

Scott Burns, "If Retirement Is So Terrible, Where Are the Riots?" 8/17/2014, https://scottburns.com/if-retirement-is-so-terrible-where-are-the-riots/

SOURCES AND REFERENCES

Aon Consulting, "2008 Replacement Ratio Study," https://www.aon.com/about-aon/intellectual-capital/attachments/human-capital-consulting/RRStudy070308.pdf

Andrew G. Biggs and Glenn R. Springstead, "Alternate Rates for Social Security Benefits and Retirement Income," 10/2008, https://www.aon.com/about-aon/intellectual-capital/attachments/human-capital-consulting/RRStudy070308.pdf

Inside Edition, "Ole Miss Freshman Hire Interior Decorator for Dorm Room," YouTube, https://www.youtube.com/watch?v=P9EERqeQhZM

MIT Living Wage Calculator, https://livingwage.mit.edu

National Vital Statistics Reports, "United States Life Tables, 2018," 11/17/2020, https://www.cdc.gov/nchs/data/nvsr/nvsr69/nvsr69-12-508.pdf

Pew Research Center, "Trends in Income and Wealth Inequality," 1/9/2020, https://www.pewresearch.org/social-trends/2020/01/09/trends-in-income-and-wealth-inequality/

"Revised Equivalence Scale: For Estimating Equivalent Incomes or Budget Costs by Family Type," 11/1968, https://fraser.stlouisfed.org/files/docs/publications/bls/bls_1570-2_1968.pdf

Social Security, "Social Security Beneficiaries by Benefit Level," https://www.ssa.gov/oact/ProgData/benefitlevel.html?type=ra

Stelter, R., de la Croix, D., and Myrskyla, M. (2021). Leaders and Laggards in Life Expectancy Among European Scholars from the Sixteenth to the Early Twentieth Century. *Demography* 58 (1): 111–135. https://read.dukeupress.edu/demography/article/58/1/111/167825/Leaders-and-Laggards-in-Life-Expectancy-Among.

USDA Food and Nutrition Service, "The Cost of Raising a Child Graphic," https://fns-prod.azureedge.us/sites/default/files/resource-files/crc_infographic-2015.2.pdf

USDA Food and Nutrition Service, "Expenditures on Children by Families," 11/26/2024, https://www.fns.usda.gov/research/cnpp/expenditures-children-families

CHAPTER FOUR

THE BIG SAMENESS IN CASH: THE REVERSE ENGINEERING WAY

Few new truths have ever won their way against the resistance of established ideas save by being overstated.

—Isaiah Berlin

The financial services industry has spent decades showing clients models that overstate retirement income needs. It all starts from a simple, but utterly wrong-headed, assertion.

To retire successfully, they say, we need to start with our preretirement earnings. Then we must figure out how to save and invest enough to replace those earnings with the money we've accumulated. The replacement rate we need, they tell us, is generally 70–80 percent of our final earnings.

One reason they do this is convention. Social Security calculates benefits as a percentage of our earnings. But not our final or last three years of earnings, our inflation-adjusted *lifetime* earnings. Quite different from final earnings.

Private and public pensions typically calculate our pension benefits as a percentage of our final earnings, usually averaged over the last three years.

So, our broker friends look studious as they give us the bad news: we aren't saving enough. Somberly, they tell us that we'll have to save more, take more risk, or both. Otherwise, our standard of living will decline the week we retire.

That's when we're tempted to say, as others have joked, "My retirement will be fine as long as I die by Friday."

NEVER MENTIONED

The same studious brokers never mention the feedback loop between savings and retirement income. If you save 20 percent of your income you don't have to replace 100 percent because you've never had 100 percent to spend. You've only had 80 percent.

At most.

But this works nicely for purported financial advisors. By getting us to save more, they increase the assets they are gathering for their firm. That means more opportunity to extract fees. And by getting us to take more risk, they move our money into something that is managed by wise and extremely well-compensated wizards who know where stock prices are headed. It works for them. It works for their firm.

Two out of three ain't bad. Sorry about you . . .

WHY THE 70 TO 80 PERCENT FIGURE IS WRONG

For most of us – and I mean about 94 percent of us – that 70–80 percent replacement rate figure simply isn't true. It isn't true even if we ignore the big life cycle effects.

To show you why, we're going to peel an onion. We're going to do it carefully, in spite of Isaiah Berlin's explicit blessing.

The first level of the onion is the interaction among our income, our savings, our insurance and work costs, and our tax bill when we retire:

- Once retired, we no longer need to save, so our 401(k) or 403(b) plan contributions go away.
- We no longer pay the employment tax because (ha-ha!) we aren't employed.
- Our health insurance bill usually goes down because we have, or will soon have, Medicare.
- Our spending for work goes down because we no longer have the clothing, commuting, lunches, and other expenses associated with having a job.

All of this was considered in a reverse-engineering project led by Bruce Palmer at Georgia State University in 1998. In addition to considering the disappearance or change in all the expenses just listed, Palmer also included an estimate of a workers Social Security benefit, assuming a steady work history. Table 4.1 shows his figures for incomes between $20,000 and $90,000.

If those seem like low wages, they aren't. They are from another century. To put it in some perspective, the Social Security wage-base maximum – the highest level of earnings subject to the employment tax – was $68,400 in that year.

Typically, about 94 percent of all earners have earnings under the wage-base maximum. So, a high-income earner with a $60,000–$70,000 salary only needed to replace 67 percent of preretirement earnings. Social Security, Palmer figured, would replace 31–36 percent. The actual income that needed to be replaced from savings and investments clocks in at 32–36 percent.

And we've just gotten started!

Table 4.1   Income Replacement Ratios for One-Earner Families.

Preretirement Income	Retirement Income	Retirement as Percentage of Preretirement	Social Security	Remaining Income to Be Replaced	Percentage
$20,000	$16,753	84	$12,342 (62%)	$4,411	22
$25,000	$20,061	80	$14,322 (57%)	$5,739	23
$30,000	$23,158	77	$16,319 (54%)	$6,839	23
$40,000	$28,873	72	$19,305 (48%)	$9,568	24
$50,000	$34,483	69	$20,444 (41%)	$14,039	28
$60,000	$40,390	67	$21,384 (36%)	$19,006	32
$70,000	$46,923	67	$21,929 (31%)	$24,994	36
$80,000	$54,651	68	$21,962 (27%)	$32,689	41
$90,000	$64,066	71	$21,995 (24%)	$42,071	47

SOURCE: Georgia State University/RETIRE Project.

THAT THING CALLED DEBT

The other procedural reason to reduce our intended income replacement rate in retirement is debt. No doubt you've heard of it. Most of us carry debt at some point in our lives. Many carry student debt. Others borrow to buy cars. Aspiring homeowners all look forward to assuming the largest debt most people ever take on: a home mortgage.

Your friendly lender will happily provide guidance about the amount of money you can borrow. Bankers have a rule of thumb for this. It's called the *28/36 rule.* The maximum amount of your income that you can spend for mortgage, insurance, and taxes is 28 percent. Another 8 percent is allowed for your "back-end ratio," the total amount of other committed payments.

That 8 percent is often the debt that prevents would-be homeowners from buying the home of their dreams. Here's a simple example. Imagine a couple with a combined income of $140,000. Both own a recently purchased car that they deem necessary for commuting.

The maximum they can spend beyond their home mortgage is $11,200 a year (8 percent of $140,000). That is about $5,600 per car or $466.67 a month. That, in turn, translates into a $24,140 car loan for 60 months or a $28,160 car loan for 72 months. I'm assuming a loan rate of 6 percent, a rate obtainable at some credit unions.

Few people carry debt that consumes 36 percent of their income for their entire working lifetime. Rising wages reduce the burden over 30 years. And many couples discover a way to finance one car at a time. They may also discover the beauty of my wife's favorite car brand, the beloved "no payment."

Many people – as singles or couples – hope to enter retirement with no mortgage debt and owning a recent model car, free and clear. Let's see how these appropriate reductions effect the replacement rate:

- Financial services industry rate: 80 percent
- Reverse engineering adjustment: minus 22 percent

- Lifetime average debt service adjustment: minus 10 to 18 percent
- Life cycle/child-rearing adjustment: minus about 20 percent
- Net replacement rate required: 28 to 20 percent
- Social Security likely to replace: 25 to 40 percent

These are broad brush figures. They tell us that recognizing normal human life and adjusting for debt, taxes, and saving can cut our real-life retirement replacement income need in half. Indeed, the real-life replacement rate is so low that Social Security benefits alone may be enough to sustain retirement.

NOT EVEN HALF CRAZY

Is that crazy? Given the amount of marketing propaganda to the contrary, we're inclined to think so. But consider this. According to the Social Security Trustees, the replacement rate (as they calculate it) for a typical median income worker is 40 percent. The replacement rate for workers at lower income levels is higher.

In addition, a major study of "alternate replacement rates" for Social Security benefits done by Andrew R. Biggs and Glenn R. Springstead in 2008 found that replacement rates were at least 100 percent across all income levels when sources of income like work earnings, pensions, and income from financial assets were considered.

It's just possible that retirement isn't an endless future of diluted tomato soup and saltine crackers.

Our most basic life decisions have an enormous impact on how much we need in savings to finance a happy retirement. The evidence, which includes a lack of rioting by well-fed retirees, suggests that real life is on our side. Unfortunately, the financial services industry isn't.

THE RETIREMENT SMILE

Still more suggests we need a lot less money in retirement than we've been told. It's called *the retirement smile.*

That's what David Blanchett, a researcher then at Morningstar, called a curious finding in his analysis of consumer spending in retirement. Examining spending patterns as people age in 2013, Blanchett found that spending peaks before retirement. In fact, for most people it peaks in their fifties, often prime earning years. After that, spending in virtually all categories declines year after year. Total spending bottoms in the early eighties, nearly three decades later.

Once in our eighties, spending starts to rise again as medical and health care spending increases. As a curve, it looks like a big wide smile.

Blanchett wasn't the first to see this. A 1999 research paper by two associate professors at Widener University, Kenn Tacchino and Cynthia Saltzman, asked a fundamental question: Do people really try to sustain the same standard of living through their later years?

Tacchino had a quick answer when I asked what caused him to research the question. "I've been teaching and working in the retirement field a long time and I can see the deficiencies in the accumulation models. It just isn't true that people consume at the same rate all their lives. At some point, usually in their eighties, the retiree settles into a sedentary life. Put it this way: next time you are on a jet plane, look around for the 80-year-olds."

A few years later, in 2005, financial planner Ty Bernicke wrote about "reality retirement planning." He noted that the 2002 Consumer Expenditure Survey showed that average annual expenditures fell from $44,330 for people 55 to 64 to only $23,759 for those over age 75.

That's an impressive drop.

The decline was not forced. Bernicke did what Tacchino and Saltzman did: He checked to see what was happening to net worth over the same period. It was *rising*, not falling. Bernicke also found a broader implication. While conventional financial planning assumptions led to a high probability of running out of money, introducing reality retirement planning assumptions showed that his clients could save less and still be assured of not running out of money. That's an inconvenient truth for the marketers of financial products.

This brings us to an awkward question. Has the financial services industry been lying since before you were born?

It looks that way. But they would just say they were exercising "an abundance of caution."

Should we be angry that we've been so misled and misinformed by people who traded on our trust? I think so. But anger won't improve your finances.

It's time to start working on a response that's positive for us. I call it *living well is the best revenge.*

RELATED COLUMNS

Scott Burns, "Life of Riley Index, Retiree Version," 10/27/1998, https://scottburns.com/the-life-of-riley-index-retiree-version-2/

Scott Burns, "Introducing the 94 Percent," 2/13/2004, https://scottburns.com/introducing-the-94-percent/

Scott Burns, "Future Retirees Will Pay More in Taxes," 4/10/2005, https://scottburns.com/future-retirees-will-pay-more-taxes/

Scott Burns, "If Retirement Is So Terrible, Where Are the Riots?," 8/17/2014, https://scottburns.com/if-retirement-is-so-terrible-where-are-the-riots/

SOURCES AND REFERENCES

Aon Consulting, "2008 Replacement Ratio Study," https://www.aon.com/about-aon/intellectual-capital/attachments/human-capital-consulting/RRStudy070308.pdf

David Blanchett, CFA, CFP, "Estimating the True Cost of Retirement," 1/2014 presentation at the Living to 100 Symposium, https://www.soa.org/globalassets/assets/files/resources/essays-monographs/2014-living-to-100/mono-li14-1a-blanchett.pdf

Andrew G. Biggs and Glenn R. Springstead, "Alternate Rates for Social Security Benefits and Retirement Income," 10/2008, https://www.aon.com/about-aon/intellectual-capital/attachments/human-capital-consulting/RRStudy070308.pdf

Inside Edition, "Ole Miss Freshman Hire Interior Decorator for Dorm Room," YouTube, https://www.youtube.com/watch?v=P9EERqeQhZM

National Vital Statistics Reports, "United States Life Tables, 2018," 11/17/2020, https://www.cdc.gov/nchs/data/nvsr/nvsr69/nvsr69-12-508.pdf

Pew Research Center, "Trends in Income and Wealth Inequality," 1/9/2020, https://www.pewresearch.org/social-trends/2020/01/09/trends-in-income-and-wealth-inequality/

Stelter, R., de la Croix, D., and Myrskyla, M. (2021). Leaders and Laggards in Life Expectancy Among European Scholars from the Sixteenth to the Early Twentieth Century. *Demography* 58 (1): 111–135. https://read.dukeupress.edu/demography/article/58/1/111/167825/Leaders-and-Laggards-in-Life-Expectancy-Among.

CHAPTER FIVE

THE SNATCH DEFEAT FROM THE JAWS OF VICTORY INDUSTRY

The supreme art of war is to subdue the enemy without fighting.
—Sun Tzu, *The Art of War*

M any in print media like to make snide references to the shallowness of their on-camera competition. "If it bleeds, it leads," they snarl, quivering at the bathos of TV news.

In fact, all of us media folks have a problem. We can't stand happiness. If it isn't a problem, it isn't interesting. We need to be serious. We prefer end-of-life-as-we-know-it events. We can look at any positive event and turn it into an earth-shattering disaster.

TURNING MORE INTO LESS

My favorite case in point is longevity. We humans have longed to have more time to live for thousands of years. Yet life was tragically short for most of us until the mid-1800s. That's when improvements in housing, sanitation, and education started to reduce the number of deaths among children and extended the lives of older people.

When the chancellor of Germany, Otto von Bismarck, called for the first government-sponsored retirement pension in 1889, it was almost a cruel joke. The pension started at age 65. But in 1890, the life expectancy of a German citizen at birth was 40.32 years.

To be sure, not all Germans died at that age. Life expectancy is not a date of death. It's the age at which *half* of all those born in a particular year could be expected to have died. The other half lives longer, with some lingering quite a while. Bismarck himself died at 83. A demographic study found that scholars in the period between 1850 and 1899 could be expected to live 69.2 years. Among philosophers, Friedrich Nietzsche missed the boat, dying in 1900 at 55. Composer Richard Wagner also missed the boat, dying at age 69 in 1883. So did Johannes Brahms. He died at 63 in 1897.

Although human life expectancy started to improve greatly in the twentieth century, the idea of a retirement pension was still a cruel joke for most people. As recently as 1940, the life expectancy of a typical American was still under 65 years. That also happens to be the year I was born. While the life expectancy of all Americans, male and female, was 62.9 years, my life expectancy as a male was 60.7 years. (I am very grateful expectancy is a median, not a hard number!)

Table 5.1   The Gift of Life, Extended.

Year	Life Expectancy
1900	47.3
1910	50.0
1920	54.1
1930	59.7
1940	62.9
1950	68.2
1960	65.7
1970	70.8
1980	73.7
1990	75.4
2000	76.8
2010	78.7
2018	78.7
2021	76.4

Sources: Adapted from https://www.cdc.gov/nchs/data/nvsr/nvsr69/nvsr69-12-508.pdf (1900–2018) and https://www.cdc.gov/nchs/data/nvsr/nvsr72/nvsr72-12.pdf (2021)

Table 5.1 shows what the broadest (male and female combined) life expectancy figures look like since 1900, by decade year, for the entire US population. Other measures show major differences. Women have higher expectancies than men. Life expectancies also vary by race, not to mention education and lifetime income.

If you are a card-carrying member of the glass-half-empty club (a requirement for media jobs), you'll focus on observing that life expectancy in the United States appears to have peaked around 2000. More recently, it got whacked by COVID-19. Looking further, you'll see that Princeton demographer Angus Deaton and his wife have seen rising "deaths of despair" among the poor and those with little education. The figures, in fact, are appalling.

Yes, I've written a bunch about this. My glass-half-empty club card is tattered with use. But without changes in our diet, revamping and renewal of public health, and more attention to pride in work, it appears that we, as a nation, have disconnected from other industrial nations. While their life expectancies continue to advance, ours appears to have gone into reverse for most of our population. Literal decades of advances in life expectancy have been lost.

THE LONGER VIEW

On the glass-half-full club side, however, the broad brush strokes are fabulous. In the last century, our group life expectancy went from 47.3 years to 76.8 years, a gain of nearly three decades, 29.5 years. That change transforms life as we live it. Is there anything better we could ask for?

Anything?

But instead of joyously celebrating, how does our society respond? Instead of asking, positively, what should we do to enjoy life for an additional three decades, we forget the joy entirely. We turn having a longer life into a grave financial problem.

Our politicians make promises to preserve Social Security, but they've taken no actions to that end since 1983. And when it comes to saving and investing, it's only a financial problem for the media. Ditto the financial services industry. Both work constantly to renew our fears.

But the problem isn't as big as the media and financial services industry has made it. So why are financial services and media so well aligned?

Upton Sinclair explained it long ago: "It is difficult to get a man to understand something, when his salary depends on his not understanding it."

Fortunately, we can subdue our combined enemies by doing as little as possible. We don't have to fight. All we need do is ignore the constant rumblings and threats and invest as simply as possible.

RELATED COLUMNS

Scott Burns, "Hey, Take the Day Off," 7/5/1998, https://scottburns.com/hey-take-the-day-off/

Scott Burns, "Life of Riley Index, Retiree Version," 10/27/1998, https://scottburns.com/the-life-of-riley-index-retiree-version-2/

Scott Burns, "Introducing the 94 Percent," 2/13/2004, https://scottburns.com/introducing-the-94-percent/

Scott Burns, "Future Retirees Will Pay More in Taxes," 4/10/2005, https://scottburns.com/future-retirees-will-pay-more-taxes/

Scott Burns, "Why Young Families Are Always Broke," 8/21/2005, https://scottburns.com/why-young-families-are-always-broke/

Scott Burns, "Why Divorce Will Lower Your Standard of Living," 9/3/2006, https://scottburns.com/why-divorce-will-lower-your-standard-of-living/

Scott Burns, "If Retirement Is So Terrible, Where Are the Riots?," 8/17/2014, https://scottburns.com/if-retirement-is-so-terrible-where-are-the-riots/

Scott Burns, "Living on Social Security in Texas," 3/13/2023, https://scottburns.com/living-on-social-security-in-texas/

SOURCES AND REFERENCES

Anne Case and Angus Deaton discuss deaths of despair, Center for the Economics of Human Development, University of Chicago, https://cehd.uchicago.edu/?p=2796

Aon Consulting, "2008 Replacement Ratio Study," https://www.aon.com/about-aon/intellectual-capital/attachments/human-capital-consulting/RRStudy070308.pdf

Andrew G. Biggs and Glenn R. Springstead, "Alternate Rates for Social Security Benefits and Retirement Income," 10/2008, https://www.aon.com/about-aon/intellectual-capital/attachments/human-capital-consulting/RRStudy070308.pdf

Inside Edition, "Ole Miss Freshman Hire Interior Decorator for Dorm Room," YouTube, https://www.youtube.com/watch?v=P9EERqeQhZM

MIT Living Wage Calculator, https://livingwage.mit.edu

National Vital Statistics Reports, "United States Life Tables, 2018," 11/17/2020, https://www.cdc.gov/nchs/data/nvsr/nvsr69/nvsr69-12-508.pdf

Pew Research Center, "Trends in Income and Wealth Inequality," 1/9/2020, https://www.pewresearch.org/social-trends/2020/01/09/trends-in-income-and-wealth-inequality/

"Revised Equivalence Scale: For Estimating Equivalent Incomes or Budget Costs by Family Type," 11/1968, https://fraser.stlouisfed.org/files/docs/publications/bls/bls_1570-2_1968.pdf

Social Security, "Social Security Beneficiaries by Benefit Level," https://www.ssa.gov/oact/ProgData/benefitlevel.html?type=ra

Stelter, R., de la Croix, D., and Myrskyla, M. (2021). Leaders and Laggards in Life Expectancy Among European Scholars from the Sixteenth to the Early Twentieth Century. *Demography* 58 (1): 111–135. https://read.dukeupress.edu/demography/article/58/1/111/167825/Leaders-and-Laggards-in-Life-Expectancy-Among.

USDA Food and Nutrition Service, "The Cost of Raising a Child Graphic," https://fns-prod.azureedge.us/sites/default/files/resource-files/crc_infographic-2015.2.pdf

USDA Food and Nutrition Service, "Expenditures on Children by Families," 11/26/2024, https://www.fns.usda.gov/research/cnpp/expenditures-children-families

CHAPTER SIX

THE SUBLIME BLESSING OF DEATH

Whoever is not in his coffin and the dark grave, let him know he has enough.

—Walt Whitman

I'm thankful that I'm not a vampire. You should be, too.

Allure of Anne Rice's epic characters notwithstanding, vampires carry a burden we normies seldom consider. With no more than a regular supply of human blood, they'll never die.

So, if they have no qualms of conscience (and don't get caught) they can dispatch as many of us as necessary to continue their existence. Some think they've got it made.

Not so.

Vampires have a big investment problem. They need to accumulate enough investment money to provide a generous income that will last forever.

VAMPIRES CAN NEVER HAVE ENOUGH

Why do they need a generous income? Simple. They can't be employees because employees don't control their work hours. One day off the night shift and they're toast due to their allergy to sunlight. And tell me what being, in their right mind, would choose to work 9 to 5 forever?

More to the point: What vampire would choose to be poor forever?

Vampires do what they gotta do.

We normies, however, have a guaranteed way out. We die.

More important, since death is natural and inevitable for normies, our savings and investment problem is way easier than the problem faced by your average vampire.

Let's compare.

Vampires invest under difficult circumstances. They need liquid and transportable assets in the event they are ever discovered or caught drinking blood. Their ownership must be indirect, lest someone notice they have failed to age. Given the horizon of their investment, it must be government proof and currency proof. And it can't be caught up, and destroyed, in the churn of human invention.

That's a tall order.

But it gets worse. In the current market, domestic equities have a dividend yield of only 1.2 percent. Inflation-protected bonds have a real yield of only 2 percent. This means a vampire would need somewhere between 83 times and 50 times whatever amount of income they wanted to avoid adding the indignity of work to the unrelenting burden of finding a blood source that will not be missed.

WHAT MERE MORTALS NEED

Mere mortals like you and me, however, need only 21 times whatever amount of income we need in retirement if Bill Bengen's classic "safe max" figure is correct, 20 times if we round up, or about 17 times if we make an annuity assumption, looking to enjoy a lifetime income but die broke. Our human figures are lower because, well, no one gets out alive.

More accurately, if we live to age 65 (as most do) we're being cautious if we assume we need to finance another 35 years of living without working. While the US population of centenarians is expected to reach 600,000 by 2050 – enough to populate Washington, DC – they will still be a small portion of our total population. The important fact here is that we humans don't need anywhere near the financial resources required to live a pleasant vampire existence.

That doesn't mean we can't quibble.

THE LIFE EXPECTANCY GAP

In public health circles, for instance, the biggest discussion in recent years has been how life expectancies vary with income and education. While the life expectancy gap between the rich and/or well educated and the poor/less educated was shrinking in the immediate post-war period, in recent years the gap has grown, indicating a kind of winner-take-all economy. The winners have education, greater income, greater wealth, and longer lives. The losers die, younger and younger.

There is zero hyperbole in any of those statements.

I first noticed this decades ago when I examined the survivorship figures for my class at MIT. We were, it turned out, dying at a very restrained pace, about five years behind the rate of the general population. I repeated the exercise at the 40th reunion. The benefits of being a nerd continued.

Those benefits, however, are well short of immortality. David Koch, who ranked high on the Forbes 400 list while he was alive, was in my class. He died in 2019 at age 79, 57 years after graduation.

Fortunately, it isn't necessary to go to MIT to enjoy living longer. According to the actuaries at Social Security, just being in the top half of the wage base gives an edge of five years over those in the bottom half. The basic recipe for longevity is more education than most: a job that provides an above-average income and a degree of personal autonomy.

But none of us get to be immortal.

Judging by the massive efforts to extend human life that are reported on daily, lots of people would happily trade the ease of financial planning of humans for the problems of immortality.

Too bad for them.

RELATED COLUMN

Scott Burns, "The Wealthy Vampire," 10/31/2010, https://scottburns.com/the-wealthy-vampire/

SOURCE AND REFERENCE

Sharmila Choudhury, Katelin P. Isaacs, Zhe Li, and Isaac A. Nicchitta, "The Growing Gap in Life Expectancy by Income: Recent Evidence and Implications for the Social Security Retirement Age," 7/06/2021, https://www.congress.gov/crs-product/R44846

PART II

THE LONG, GLORIOUS HISTORY OF INVESTMENT FAILURE

CHAPTER SEVEN

WESTON WELLINGTON AND THE WISDOM OF NOT GUESSING THE FUTURE

Investing should be more like watching paint dry or watching grass grow. If you want excitement, take $800 and go to Las Vegas.

—Paul Samuelson, 1970 Nobel laureate in economics

T he building is a tall, graceful arc of glass. Think future world. It is perched on an escarpment overlooking Texas Loop 360 and the magnificent topography of Austin. It is the headquarters of Dimensional Fund Advisors.

I've come here to visit with Weston Wellington. His job, since before the dawn of digital history, has been to communicate the magic of the Dimensional Fund way to normal humans. Doing this takes him to conferences and client meetings around the world. In the last year he has clocked over 120 flight segments. He loves it.

Once a devoted New Englander with Mayflower roots, he is now an advanced tri-coastal being. He has places on the East and West Coast, an apartment in Austin, and enough frequent flyer points to be sublimely comfortable wherever his flights take him.

He's also funny, in a whimsical, sardonic way. That's one of the reasons I've been looking forward to this visit. While I've heard his presentations many times, it has always been from a lecture hall seat, looking down from a high row. This time we'll be meeting eye-to-eye, two old guys who feel at ease remembering what happened in 1974 or 1987 or some other year close to the beginning of time.

THE GROWTH OF AN IDEA, IN BILLIONS

Armed with only a bachelor's degree in English, Wellington tells the tale of how devoted academics started the firm in 1984 and grew it to become a major asset management firm. As of 2024, the firm has over $786 billion in assets under management (AUM in finance speak), spread over mutual funds and exchange-traded funds. It's also home to some 1,600 employees, most of whom have at least an MBA degree. Many have PhDs, with enough of them together to make you think of the entire floors of PhDs at places like Intel, AMD, Apple, and Nvidia.

This is not your everyday mix of people.

Go to one of the firms' regular conferences and you'll be scheduled for a day of intense, back-to-back lecture/slide shows. Featured topics: statistics, probability, and itsy-bitsy investment details. You'll learn (or be reminded) that Dimensional is not an index investing company, despite the multitudes who refer to it that way.

Dimensional doesn't invest to follow an existing index like the S&P 500 or the Russell 2000. It doesn't buy and sell company stocks as they enter or fall out of the prescribed list.

No, it is an "asset class" investing company. Dimensional works assiduously to assemble portfolios of stocks that represent the characteristics of an asset class. They do it in the most efficient way possible. Then, with a full basket of asset class funds, portfolio managers can assemble the most risk/reward-efficient portfolio possible.

Yes, very tedious stuff.

J. ALFRED PRUFROCK, ADVENTURER

No romance. No swashbucklers. Just the unrelenting statistics and equations nerds love. Risk is so frequent a topic that T. S. Eliot's J. Alfred Prufrock is an adventurer by comparison.

But the scholarly stuff doesn't end there. Just to make sure you really get their academic roots, you might get to hear Eugene F. Fama, the University of Chicago finance professor at the Booth School of Business who won his Nobel laureate in economics in 2013. Or Dartmouth's Kenneth French who co-developed the three-factor model with Fama. Or MIT's Robert C. Merton who won his Nobel laureate in economics in 1997.

And, lest you forget, the founder of Dimensional was a student of Fama's. David Booth's pledge of $300 million to Chicago's business school is stunning. Just to compare in Texas giantism, Red McCombs's $50 million dollar gift to the McCombs School of Business at the University of Texas, Austin, was record setting. People called it *transformative*.

So, what, exactly, does Weston Wellington do?

STAY IN YOUR SEAT

Follow me.

After entering the building, a security person copies my driver's license information. He gives me a visitor's pass, which takes me through the security turnstile. I follow Wellington up to the fourth floor. He quickly grabs his laptop from an open space work desk. I follow him to a small conference room.

"A lot of what I do is keeping track of the forecasts people make. Basically, I look for bookends – extreme prediction," he says. He's been doing this for decades, so he has a rich, long history to talk about.

The most famous, by far, is the 1979 *Business Week* cover proclaiming "the Death of Equities."

But there are so many more. His open laptop screen is covered with dozens of icons for magazine and newspaper stories making extreme statements.

"It's a target-rich environment," he smiles.

He explains that he has two general approaches. But he favors one that's about the futility of market timing. He calls it *stay in your seat*.

He starts with 1970:

- June 1970 *Time* magazine cover. It is a picture of Federal Reserve Chairman Arthur Burns. A slanted yellow banner asks, "Is this slump necessary?" Under his name another banner declares, "Facing an Economy on the Brink."

- November 1973 *Time* magazine cover. It's a picture of Saudi King Feisal labeled "The Hand on the Valve." A white banner slants across the top: "The Oil Squeeze." Inside, the magazine said, "Not since World War II has any event carried more potential for global change," referencing the first OPEC oil embargo.
- August 1974 is a *New York Times* front page. "Nixon Resigns" He is the first to "quit his post."
- September 1974 is another *Time* cover showing a cartoon head with an ice bag on top and a thermometer. Its slanted green banner says, "The Big Headache." Inside it refers to ". . . an economy that seems out of control."
- October 1975 is a *New York Daily News* front page. "Ford to City: Drop Dead." A subhead says the former vice president who became president when Nixon resigned "Vows He'll Veto Any Bail-Out."
- August 1979 is the *Business Week* cover showing crumpled stock certificates. The famous headline reads: "The Death of Equities: How Inflation Is Destroying the Stock Market."

Starting with an investment of $100,000 in January 1970 Wellington points out, your money would have grown to $176,760 in the S&P 500 Index and $184,300 invested in one-month Treasury bills by the end of 1979. That's no reward for risk relative to riskless Treasuries. And, sorry, no adjustment for inflation.

"But stay in your seat," he says calmly. He's just warming up. He has another four decades of headlines:

- March 1980 in a picture of the Hunt brothers, hands raised to give testimony after their failed attempt to corner the silver market. The *New York Times* story declares ". . . the sharpest sustained retreat since the disastrous summer of 1974."
- August 1983 is another *New York Times* story in which John Kenneth Galbraith predicts, "A renewal of inflation . . ." and Milton Friedman predicts, "Interest rates will rise."

- May 1984 is an Associated Press story in the *New York Times* with a picture of Salomon Brothers chief economist Henry Kaufman. The story quotes him as saying, "Interest rates to move spectacularly higher." (Mind you, Kaufman wasn't just anyone. Back then when he spoke, markets moved.)
- October 1987 is a *Time* magazine cover emblazoned "The Crash: After a wild week on Wall Street, the world is different." That one-day crash is now called *the flash crash*.
- September 1989 is a *Fortune* magazine cover story with Sony Chairman Akio Morita staring at us holding a filmless camera. "Where Japan Will Strike Next: In electronics, financial services, retailing, supercomputers – here comes the broadest export push yet."

As ever, lots to worry about. "But look what happened over the decade," Wellington smiles. He clicks to another slide. From January 1970 to December 1989, $100,000 invested in the S&P 500 grew to $891,031 while the same amount in riskless one-month Treasury bills rose to only $432,000. Again, not adjusted for inflation.

Wellington, moving faster and faster, clicked through the nineties, the aughts, and the tens at a near manic pace.

THE HUGE BOTTOM LINE

But I'll be a spoiler here.

Slide please.

From January 1970 through December 2020, $100,000 invested in the S&P 500 grew to (are you ready?) $18,208,146. That's a rather impressive reward for patience and sloth.

And the one-month Treasuries? Well, they had grown to $969,979.

Wellington smiled.

"Stay in your seat," he said.

There are some due diligence techno-quibbles here. Neither figure is adjusted for inflation. And the stock growth isn't adjusted for taxes on capital gains as well as dividends. Or the cost of management.

Even so, the reward for doing as little as humanly possible is clear.

RELATED COLUMN

Scott Burns, "The Portfolio of Nobel Prize Winners," 8/3/1999, https://scott burns.com/the-portfolio-of-nobel-prize-winners/

SOURCES AND REFERENCES

Dimensional Funds Website, "About Us," https://www.dimensional.com/us-en/who-we-are/about-us

Eugene F. Fama, bio at the Chicago Booth School of Business, https://www.chicagobooth.edu/faculty/directory/f/eugene-f-fama

Kenneth R. French, bio at Dartmouth's Tuck School of Business, https://mba.tuck.dartmouth.edu/pages/faculty/ken.French/index.html

Robert C. Merton, official website, https://robertcmerton.com

John Rekenthaler, "More Lessons from the Do Nothing Portfolio," 4/20/2023, https://www.morningstar.com/columns/rekenthaler-report/more-lessons-do-nothing-portfolio

CHAPTER EIGHT

THE LEGION OF AMAZING, BUT TEMPORARY, HEROES

Ultimately, nothing should be more important to investors than the ability to sleep soundly at night.

—Seth Klarman

Investing history is littered with fallen heroes. Once declared legends in the battle against the market, their moment of failure comes when the fund they manage suddenly stumbles. Then the fund falls, trounced by the index it is pitted against.

What's seldom mentioned is that the fallen hero has retired to his vineyard in Sonoma, to somewhere in the Hamptons, to a 10,000 square foot log cabin in Jackson Hole, or some other place that normal humans would call close to heaven.

Some of the fallen don't even move far away.

When I lived in Boston, I was always amazed at the number of money managers who lived in long, posh lines in places like Eastern Point on the Boston north shore. Others went further south, lining the beachfront and view parcels in places like Nantucket.

The reason for this is simple. Money managers are well compensated – sometimes hysterically well compensated – for taking risks with our money. So, it's kind of like the country and western song except it's not an ex-wife that gets the gold mine, and we get the shaft. The managers don't lose *their* money. They lose *our* money.

Despite that dismal reality, money managers are habitually portrayed as fighters. They are modern heroic figures. They battle alone against an intractable, unpredictable, and treacherous foe. We engage the money manager, they take up sword and shield for us, and they set out to kill the dragon.

It makes a good story.

And that's how it will appear, whether it shows up in *Money*, *Kiplinger's*, *Forbes*, or *Fortune*. That's how it's done.

The reality is that heroes are like the rest of us. They make mistakes. They can make lots of money some of the time, but they can, and do, make mistakes that will lose most, or all, of the extra return they have made.

Or worse.

You don't have to take my word for this. You can find plenty of examples in a single book. In *Big Mistakes: The Best Investors and Their Worst Investments*, Michael Batnick covers more than a century of well-known investors and their biggest mistakes. Here are two.

THE HAZARDS OF GENIUS, NOT THE DUKES OF HAZARD

We don't see John Meriwether's name in print much these days but his hedge fund, Long-Term Capital Management, nearly destroyed the global finance system despite being led by a brain trust that included Nobel Prize laureates. With deep belief in their formulas and ultra-sophisticated math, the firm took leveraged positions.

The word *leveraged* doesn't express their level of risk. At one point, according to Batnick, the firm had "$1.25 *trillion* in open positions." They were levered 100:1, meaning that a 1 percent change in value would wipe out 100 percent of the firms' actual assets.

And that's what happened in September 1998.

In only five weeks, their $3.6 billion of investor capital vaporized, an amount four times larger than the next largest hedge fund at the time. As Batnick summarized the debacle, "They were able to calculate the odds of everything, but they understood the possibility of nothing."

In a world full of very bright people, many of them attracted to the investment business, just being super-smart isn't enough.

And what happened to Meriwether?

In the following year he opened a second hedge fund, starting with $250 million. It lasted a decade and closed. A third hedge fund was less successful, raising only $28 million. His Wikipedia page notes that he has also been into horse racing, a sport very few can afford.

MISTAKING A RISING MARKET FOR GENIUS

Jerold Tsai was a young Turk at Fidelity, managing Fidelity Capital Fund at age 30. He moved fast, made big trades, and made big money. From 1958 to 1965, the fund earned a 296 percent return, nearly double the 166 percent return of the average comparable fund in the same period. Everyone took note – not just fund investors, but fund managers.

Riding that wave, Tsai left Fidelity to start his own firm. His Manhattan Fund was scheduled to open with the sale of 2.5 million shares. But his fame as a brilliant manager was so great that 27 million shares were sold, bringing in $270 million. That seems a small sum these days, but this was 1966. His fund accounted for 15 percent of all new money into equity mutual funds that year. Even more incredible from today's perspective, buyers of the fund were willing to pay an 8.5 percent commission.

It didn't end well.

Manhattan Fund enjoyed an inspiring return of 40 percent in 1967 but lost 7 percent in 1968, ranking near the bottom against other managed funds. After that, it got worse. The amazing bull market of the 1950s and early 1960s hit the bear market of 1969 and 1970. Investors lost their faith in wonder stocks.

By 1974, according to Batnick, the Manhattan Fund had the worst eight-year performance in mutual fund history.

Tsai, it turned out, had ridden a rising market as aggressively as possible. He mistook a bull market for genius.

Tsai died in 2008, but he did not die poor. Before Manhattan Fund started its long decline, he sold his management company for $27 million but continued to manage the fund. In 1973, he left the company and sold his stock. He then bought a brokerage house and made a series of moves that eventually made him the largest shareholder in Primerica. He left the company with a $40 million "golden parachute" in 2000.

WAS IT SKILL OR LUCK?

The biggest question we face when selecting an investment manager seems simple. Does the manager have actual skill? Or were they just lucky? Fund advertisements like to point to the previous few years as evidence. It makes a good story, so lots of people buy based on recent information.

That's a mistake.

It takes a lot of math to sort out whether a manager is skilled or just lucky. Batnick, for instance, makes frequent references to Michael J. Mauboussin, one of the best-known researchers in skill versus luck. A more colorful researcher in the area is Annie Duke, a professional poker player known as the "Duchess of Poker."

When the math is done, the problem we face is that by the time we can be sure the manager has skill rather than luck, the opportunity is long gone. Suppose, for instance, we're watching a manager who is performing, year after year, in the top 10 to 25 percent of managers. They'd need to do that for 43 years before we could be 95 percent certain that the performance was a matter of skill. Even a sensational manager would require a period of 16 years.

So, we either guess, or we're certain to be late to the party.

Here are two examples from researcher Zhijian Wu, CEO of Woodsford, Singapore.

Peter Lynch, the famed manager of Fidelity Magellan, ran the fund from 1978 to 1990. He beat the S&P 500 almost every year. But few noticed until 1990, the year he retired. Most of the money invested in the fund went in *after* 1990, just as its performance began to sag.

Lynch moved to a higher position at Fidelity and went on to erroneously tell investors that you could withdraw 7 percent a year from your 100 percent equities retirement account and never run out of money (see Chapter 1).

Much the same happened to Bill Miller, manager of the equally famed Legg Mason Capital Management Value Trust. The fund beat the S&P 500 every year from 1991 to 2005, a sensational record. His performance indicated skill. But if you invested in his fund on that basis, you'd have lost money because fund performance reversed. From 2006 to 2011, the fund underperformed the S&P 500 every year by a wide margin, losing 70 percent of its value, according to *Institutional Investor*.

Miller retired from the fund in 2011 but went on to start his own firm and has been successful managing money on a smaller scale. You won't see his name on the *New York Times* 100 Neediest List.

THE ORIGINS OF THE INVESTOR HERO

But not to worry. It turns out that the archetype, the meme, the narrative, the "hero with a thousand faces" model for the heroic money manager was created by the man who later created and funded the equivalent of the Pulitzer Prize for financial journalism.

In the Introduction to a revised edition of his first book, *The Battle for Investment Survival*, Gerald M. Loeb wrote, "When I started investing about 1921, it seemed a peaceful enough occupation. By 1943 I started calling it a 'battle,' though a lot of people might have used that term much earlier during 1929 to 1932. But now in 1957 it seems to me a 'war.'"

In 1971, he doubled down on heroic conflict with his second book, *Your Battle for Stock Market Profits: How to Make Money and Keep It in Today's Market*.

What advice did Loeb give individual investors in his years writing a column that was syndicated by the North American Newspaper Alliance? He told readers to concentrate their investments in a handful of stocks and watch them closely.

Perhaps it worked for him.

But it seldom works for most people. For you and me, a concentrated portfolio poses the risk of a "torpedo stock" – the stock that takes down the entire portfolio and wrecks your retirement. A more common strategy is to reduce risk by diversification, hoping that you can own enough stocks to eliminate torpedo risk and achieve a market return.

How many stocks does that take? Way more than five. Some say 20 will do it. Others say 100. In fact, those are just numbers moving closer to the ideal, which is *all* stocks. In other words, an index that covers the entire market.

We know this from one of the bedrock papers in investment research, Harry Markowitz's "Portfolio Selection," published in 1952. Markowitz won the John von Neumann Theory Prize in 1989 and the Nobel Prize in 1990.

But back to Mr. Loeb.

According to Amazon, his first book is no longer in print. But it is available as a used paperback just like the yellowing copy in my personal library. Originally priced at $2.95, a copy in good condition can now be purchased from a used book dealer for $27.99. That calculates to an annual appreciation rate of 4.70 percent.

And guess what?

That 4.7 percent compares well to the annualized inflation rate, 3.9 percent over that period. That's slightly better than the 4.5 percent annualized return on riskless one-month Treasury bills.

At least the book itself wasn't a bad investment.

RELATED COLUMNS

Scott Burns, "Dangerous Advice from Peter Lynch," 10/1/1995, https://scottburns
.com/dangerous-advice-from-peter-lynch/

Scott Burns, "The Missing Bullet Holes Problem," 11/15/2015, https://scottburns
.com/the-missing-bullet-holes-problem/

SOURCES AND REFERENCES

Batnick, M. (2018). *Big Mistakes: The Best Investors and Their Worst Investments.* Wiley/Bloomberg.

Duke, A. (2018). *Thinking in Bets: Making Smarter Decisions When You Don't Have All the Facts.* Portfolio/Penguin.

Mauboussin, M.J. (2012). *The Success Equation: Untangling Skill and Luck in Business, Sports, and Investing.* Harvard Business Review Press.

Dan Weil, "Bill Miller in the Wilderness and Loving It," *Institutional Investor*, 1/23/2019, https://www.institutionalinvestor.com/article/2bswi2n30990nntbscc1s/corner-office/bill-miller-in-the-wilderness-and-loving-it

Wikipedia bio of Annie Duke, https://en.wikipedia.org/wiki/Annie_Duke

Wikipedia bio of Michael J. Mauboussin, https://en.wikipedia.org/wiki/Michael_J._Mauboussin

Zhijian Wu, "How to Tell Whether a Fund Manager is Skillful or Lucky," 10/28/2015, https://www.linkedin.com/pulse/how-tell-whether-fund-manager-skillful-lucky-伍治坚-zhijian-wu

CHAPTER NINE

BOGLEHEADS AND FIGHTING BACK

Don't look for the needle in the haystack. Just buy the haystack.
—John C. Bogle

Today, it's easy to become a Couch Potato investor. In 1991, when I first introduced the idea, it was more expensive (but still way cheap!). Then it was difficult to do. Now it can be done on virtually any major investing platform (see Chapters 12, 27, and 28 for specifics) – at least in the United States.

The hard part is staying the course. As shown in Chapters 7 and 8, we face a constant barrage of advertising, commentary, and advice telling us that change is needed, today. Others tell us this is a "stock pickers market."

Then there's the fear of missing out. If others are making dramatic amounts of money, we wish we were along for the ride. Alternatively, there is plain old fear. It keeps some cowering in cash or gold because life as we know it is about to end, as it has been for over 2,000 years.

FINDING SUPPORT

The best antidote is a support group, a haven for index investors you can visit whenever you want, wherever you are.

One is the John C. Bogle Center for Financial Literacy. Think of it as the nerve center for all Bogledom. In addition to providing information on the annual Bogleheads conference, it provides links to the 74 Bogleheads chapters around the United States and the 9 chapters in other countries. The threads enable you to ask questions and seek information from other members by region and by life stage, from just starting out in life to retired.

That's just scratching the surface.

Click a button and the site will connect you to a Bogle archive, a wiki page, a Facebook page, a YouTube page, a Twitter page, and a Reddit page. Whatever your preferred medium, it's there.

In a recent visit, the site offered these statistics for activity:

- 130,000 members
- 2 million visits per month
- 22 million pages read per month
- 7 million posts

If you want some in-person contact, you can join a chapter and attend meetings. I've been to meetings of the Austin chapter. I've enjoyed the age and experience range of the gatherings. No one is trying to sell anything. You learn a little (sometimes more than you want to know) and you enjoy the feeling of community with others who have chosen the same path.

Need some immediate encouragement?

You can always go to my website, www.scottburns.com or visit couch-potatoman on Substack. With no advertising to distract you, it offers what a restaurant would call small plates – columns that are typically 700–800 words long. You can search by topic, by month or year, or by word.

RELATED COLUMNS

Scott Burns, "Bogle Says: All Costs Matter," 10/5/1997, https://scottburns.com/bogle-says-all-costs-matter/

Scott Burns, "A Visit with John Bogle," 2/21/2010, https://scottburns.com/a-visit-with-john-bogle/

Scott Burns, "The New Skepticism," 2/22/2015, https://scottburns.com/the-new-skepticism/

Scott Burns, "The Better Monkey Solution," 3/9/2024, https://scottburns.com/the-better-monkey-solution-low-cost-index-fund-investing/

SOURCES AND REFERENCES

The Bogleheads, https://www.bogleheads.org (activity data from 6/10/25)
The Bogleheads Facebook page, https://www.facebook.com/Bogleheads/
The John C. Bogle Center for Financial Literacy, https://boglecenter.net
Scott Burns website, https://scottburns.com

CHAPTER TEN

TURN OFF, TUNE OUT, AND DROP IN (WITH APOLOGIES TO TIMOTHY LEARY)

Think for yourself. Question authority.

—Timothy Leary

T he late Harvard psychologist Timothy Leary, who advocated using LSD and other psychedelic drugs to expand consciousness, is best known for saying, "Turn on, tune in, and drop out" at a "human be-in" in early 1967.

For those of us who can remember the time, the best we can say is, "it seemed like a good idea at the time."

Back then, we had three television networks and broadcast news. The *New York Review of Books* and the *Village Voice* represented the outer reaches of the American psyche.

Get in your car and your information source was an AM–FM radio. It had a volume knob. Perhaps a half dozen preset buttons. That was it.

Today we live in what's been called *the attention economy*: an endless struggle by multitudes of people and institutions to capture our attention. The number of choices is so great we now face huge screens in our cars that have virtually nothing to do with the car or our driving. Instead, they are gateways to our unlimited listening and viewing choices.

The statistics here are astounding. According to Nielsen data, Americans 18 and over spend nearly 60 hours a week engaged with TV, internet/video on computer, and app/web on a smartphone or tablet. That's a lot of time.

It's also an enormous opportunity.

Every hour that we reclaim is an hour we can use to keep a clear head, love the people in our lives, make life a bit better for anyone we see, and focus on what we want our lives to be about.

We could do worse.

That's why we will benefit from the following:

- **Turn off** notifications.
- **Tune out** most purported information sources.
- **Drop in** to being present in the moment. As is, where is.

I'm not putting on a self-improvement guru hat here. I'll leave that to others. Instead, let's just consider the personal finance benefits.

Once you tune out:

- **You'll not be bothered** with all the conflicting voices predicting an unpredictable future.
- **You'll be able to stay in your seat.**
- **You'll enjoy the silent benefits** of low-cost index investing. They will provide you with returns almost certainly superior to 80 percent, or more, of all other investors.
- **You'll recoup hours** of otherwise wasted time.

THE BOOK YOU NEED TO READ

Want to know why you should take the red pill path? Sit down with Jaron Lanier's *Ten Arguments for Deleting Your Social Media Accounts Right Now* (Henry Holt, 2018). (And check Lanier's dust jacket picture if you want to remember the Tim Leary days.)

AND FURTHER SUPPORT READING

If you haven't thought about this for yourself or wished you could get one of your kids off their phone, here are four starter books you'll enjoy reading. All four can be read, or listened to, in less than 24 hours. The first requires less than half an hour.

- Will Regent, *Digital Minimalism: The Essential Guide to Minimizing Your Time in the Digital World, Learn Tips on How You Can Unplug and Spend More Time in the Real World* (Online Agile, 2024; listening time 26 minutes)

- Jerry Odell, *How to Do Nothing: Resisting the Attention Economy* (Melville House, 2019; listening time 8 hours and 10 minutes)
- Johann Hari, *Stolen Focus: Why You Can't Pay Attention and How to Think Deeply Again* (Crown, 2022; listening time 10 hours and 21 minutes)

RELATED COLUMNS

Scott Burns, "Return to Big Bend," 2/1/2005, https://scottburns.com/return-to-big-bend/

Scott Burns, "Enlarging the Cup of Life," 12/25/2016, https://scottburns.com/enlarging-the-cup-of-life/

Scott Burns, "A TV Epiphany," 9/23/2018, https://scottburns.com/a-tv-epiphany/

Scott Burns, "Are You Selling Your Leisure Time Too Cheap?" 11/30/2023, https://scottburns.com/are-you-selling-your-leisure-time-too-cheap/

Scott Burns, "Discovering Abundance," 8/25/2024, https://scottburns.com/discovering-abundance/

SOURCES AND REFERENCES

Backlinko, https://backlinko.com/screen-time-statistics

John C. Bogle, Center for Financial Literacy, https://boglecenter.net/resources/

PART III

HOW TO INVEST YOUR SAVINGS

CHAPTER ELEVEN

ETFS: YOU CAN NOW INVEST ALMOST FOR FREE

Change will not come if we wait for some other person or some other time. We are the ones we've been waiting for. We are the change that we seek.

—Barack Obama

In a better world, we might have started out like this. Today, at last, we can.

We can save and invest at minimal expense. We can do it on our own. You can now invest at minimal cost. You can do it from home. Or the beach. Here are the steps:

- Start an IRA brokerage account.
- Put half of your money in the Vanguard Total Stock Market Index ETF (ticker: VTI).
- Put the other half in the Vanguard Total Bond Market Index ETF (ticker: BND).

Presto, you have a Couch Potato Portfolio!

A COUCH POTATO PORTFOLIO CAN BE BUILT ANYWHERE

You can do this at Vanguard, of course. But you can also do it at Schwab, Fidelity, Merrill Lynch, Chase/JPMorgan, Wealthfront, and any number of firms that offer a self-directed brokerage account.

As different as these firms can be, here is what all now share:

- You won't pay a commission to make the purchase.
- Since ETFs trade on exchanges like stocks and bonds there is a spread between the asking price for shares and the bid price. But the spread for these two ETFs is *tiny*. It runs about 0.01 percent.
- The annual expense ratio for these ETFs is 0.03 percent. This is a fraction of the cost of the average ETF. It's also a fraction of the average expense ratio for the lifestyle (target date) mutual fund portfolios offered in most employer-sponsored retirement plans. Those declined to an average 0.30 percent in 2023, according to the Investment Company Institute. That's 10 *times* as much as the cost of the basic Couch Potato portfolio.

Indeed, that 0.03 percent is lower than the gold standard for employee retirement plan costs. That would be the Federal Thrift Savings Plan. Its funds cost 0.037 percent a year.

CALCULATING THE DIFFERENCE COSTS MAKE

If you accumulate $1 million in your IRA brokerage account with Vanguard ETFs in it, it will cost all of $300 a year.

This is dirt cheap.

Here's some perspective. In 1968, the *New York Times* celebrated the widespread ownership of common stocks through mutual funds, declaring we had entered the age of people's capitalism.

The cost of entry? Most funds had front-end commission costs of 8.5 percent. It was followed by annual expenses that could be 1.5 percent.

Had you invested $10,000 then and enjoyed a gross return of 10 percent annually, your original investment would have grown to $239,117 – if IRA retirement accounts had even existed back then.

Invest the same amount at the same gross return at today's expenses and your original investment would grow to $447,681, almost twice as much.

If you lived in a magical, cost-free world, your $10,000 would grow to $452,593. The difference between free and dirt cheap is only $4,912 of $437,681 in net gains. I don't think it can get much better than this.

A NEW AGE

We have new opportunities. ETFs are the primary tool we can use for self-directed investing.

How did this happen?

Innovation and competition, two of the really nice things about capitalism. Just as Fidelity's Ned Johnson thought he could sell more funds if he reduced, then eliminated, front-end loads. Just as Charles Schwab thought there was room for a deep discount brokerage house. Or just as State Street Global Advisors thought there was a market for an open-ended index fund that traded throughout the day.

Beginning in 1993 with a single ETF that duplicated the Standard & Poor's 500 index with the ticker SPY, the idea got off to a slow start. SPY gained $133 million in assets in the quarter it was introduced. Fully 10 years later, in 2003, assets had grown to just more than $100 billion. Even so, ETFs weren't noteworthy enough to be mentioned in the Investment Company Institutes' Annual Factbook. Eight years after that, in 2011, ETFs hit their first $1 trillion in assets.

As of April 2025, there are 3,873 ETFs in the United States. According to the Investment Company Institute, US-offered ETFs had $10.3 trillion in assets by the end of 2023.

In typical Wall Street fashion, anything worth doing will be worth doing to excess and exhaustion. New ETFs are created each year. And not-so-old ETFs are quietly closed out each year for lack of interest, poor performance, or both.

Since anyone with a computer can create an index, the number of ETFs is potentially infinite, however silly.

But all that is a sideshow.

It's the usual Wall Street experiment of throwing Jello at the wall to see if it sticks.

Couch Potato investors focus on the ETFs that are largest in assets, most traded, and lowest cost. Costs matter.

RELATED COLUMNS

Scott Burns, "The Conspiracy for Failure in 401(k) Plans," 8/23/2013, https://scottburns.com/the-conspiracy-for-failure-in-401k-plans/

Scott Burns, "The Simplicity Manifesto," 3/31/2019, https://scottburns.com/the-simplicity-manifesto/

Scott Burns, "Two Days of Truth in 365 Days of Snake Oil," 4/17/2020, https://scottburns.com/two-days-of-truth-in-365-days-of-snake-oil/

Scott Burns, "SPIVA: The Investment News That's No Longer News," 6/19/2022, https://scottburns.com/index-funds-beat-managed-funds-again-and-again/

SOURCES AND REFERENCES

ETF Asset Growth, https://fred.stlouisfed.org/series/BOGZ1FL564090005Q

Investment Company Institute Data on Lifestyle/Target Date Mutual Fund Expense Ratios, 2023, https://www.ici.org/news-release/24-news-401k-investors

Investment Company Institute Data on Size of US ETF Market, https://www.ici.org/faqs/faqs_etfs_market#:~:text=As%20of%20December%202023%2C%20the,companies%20at%20year%2Dend%202024

Thrift Savings Plan Expenses and Fees, https://www.tsp.gov/tsp-basics/expenses-and-fees/

Vanguard Institutional Data on BND Shares Bid/Ask Spread, https://institutional.vanguard.com/investments/product-details/fund/0928

Vanguard Institutional Data on VTI Shares Bid/Ask Spread, https://institutional.vanguard.com/investments/product-details/fund/0970

Y Charts Graph of Total US ETFs, https://ycharts.com/indicators/us_number_of_etfs

CHAPTER TWELVE

THE SIMPLICITY PORTFOLIO – COUCH POTATO INVESTING

Benign neglect is the secret to long-term investing success.
—Charles Ellis

The Couch Potato portfolio that I introduced in 1991 won't provide you with the highest possible return. It's not about that. It's about simplicity. In the investment business it's called *ease of execution* – you won't find an easier, lower cost way to invest your savings whether they are in a taxable account, Roth account, IRA account, or 401(k) or 403(b) account.

Here's why:

- You don't have to do any math.
- If you hate math of any kind, you can use a pocket calculator to divide by the number 2.
- No one will know.

There will be years when your portfolio results trail an all-stock portfolio. And there will be years when your results beat an all-stock portfolio. All you will know for certain is that each of the two parts will beat most of its managed fund competitors about 80 percent of the time, sometimes by more.

Will it make you insanely rich?

No way.

But it will make you rich enough. In due course, you'll be able to stop working. You'll be able to live on what you've saved for the rest of your life.

THE EVIDENCE

The evidence supporting the superiority of low-cost index investing has been accumulating for over half a century. Most would put the genesis of the idea in the late 1960s or early 1970s. The most cited origin of the idea that professional managers won't be able to beat an index is an article written by investment consultant Charles Ellis. Published in the *Financial Analysts Journal* in 1975, "The Loser's Game" argued that most money was managed by professionals, not individuals, and that the professionals were competing against each other, not the proverbial rubes of Main Street.

The best ongoing examination of actual performance results is an exercise Standard & Poor's does twice annually: the SPIVA report (SPIVA stands for "S&P Indexes Versus Active"), While most performance measures only count *surviving* funds over a period, the SPIVA report begins with the number of funds that *started* a given period. It includes all the funds that were merged into other funds or just buried without a gravestone.

You'd be surprised at the fatality rate funds suffer. But the SPIVA report tells all, fund category by fund category. At the end of 2024, for instance, here's how managed large-cap domestic funds did relative to their index:

1 year: 34.76 percent outperformed the S&P 500

3 years: 15.04 percent outperformed the S&P 500

5 years: 23.74 percent outperformed the S&P 500

10 years: 15.66 percent outperformed the S&P 500

15 years: 10.50 percent outperformed the S&P 500

You don't have to be a Certified Financial Analyst to see that the longer the time, the fewer actively managed funds to beat the passive index they are measured against. While the exact figures change somewhat each passing year, the direction is always the same.

Similar figures apply for corporate and government bond funds:

Period	Corporate Bonds (%)	Government Bonds (%)
1 year	69.62	27.5
3 years	65.56	13.89
5 years	42.11	11.11
10 years	9.92	22.09
15 years	18.37	1.69

YOU'LL BE INVESTING FAR LONGER

This is a good time to remember that you may be investing during a career of 35 or more years. After that you'll be investing during a retirement that could last another 35 years.

So there you have it. Long-term professional management is doomed. You may need advice in other areas of personal finance, but when the guys in the fancy suspenders and expensive eyeglasses look at you and suggest that their firm's research will produce superior results, ask them about what they have been smoking.

HOW TO BE A COUCH POTATO INVESTOR AND DEAL WITH INVESTMENT TALK

Let's address the one remaining problem in your investing life and, possibly, your social life. What will you talk about in social gatherings?

How will you participate when the subject turns to investing, the markets, and the latest brilliant triumph the person who cornered you has achieved?

Since these are all status declarations, here are some suggestions:

When asked, "What do you do?" (a status bracketing question):
Answer: "In event of what?" (look bemused)

When told of a great financial gain:
Reply: "Are you *still* concerned about money?"

When regaled with a learned discussion of all measures of the money supply:
Reply: "However it's measured, there's always enough. At least for me."

When you hear a complaint about the cost of staying at the Jerome in Aspen:

Reply: "Travel just doesn't move the needle for me these days."

When the cost of, say, Wagyu or dry-aged rib-eye is mentioned:

Reply: "Really? I haven't paid attention to prices for years."

Finally, if you really need an exit strategy, try an abrupt change of subject:

Reply: "The discord you feel reminds me of a famous poetry line, "Even the Bauds of Euphony would cry out sharply.""

This will clear space around you quicker than a request for a cash donation.

RELATED COLUMN

Scott Burns columns on SPIVA, https://scottburns.com/?s=%22SPIVA%22

SOURCES AND REFERENCES

Charles Ellis, "The Losers Game," *Financial Analysts Journal*, https://www
    .tandfonline.com/doi/epdf/10.2469/faj.v31.n4.19?needAccess=true
SPIVA reports, https://www.spglobal.com/spdji/en/research-insights/spiva/

CHAPTER THIRTEEN

OCCAM'S RAZOR: RIFFS ON THE COUCH POTATO PORTFOLIO THAT DON'T WORK

True story, Word of Honor:
Joseph Heller, an important and funny writer,
now dead, and I were at a party given by a billionaire

on Shelter Island.
I said, "Joe, how does it make you feel
to know that our host only yesterday
may have made more money
than your novel Catch-22
has earned in its entire history?"
And Joe said, "I've got something he can never have."
And I said, "What on earth could that be, Joe?"
And Joe said, "The knowledge that I've got enough."
Not bad! Rest in Peace!"
    —Kurt Vonnegut, *The New Yorker Magazine*, May 2005

Jack Bogle founded Vanguard. He is the father of low-cost index investing. He was also a fan of Occam's razor.

So are Couch Potato investors, even if they've never heard of it.

Occam's razor is a principle, often unheeded, named after William of Occam. He was a fourteenth-century English philosopher and theologian.

Here's the principle: If many explanations or solutions are offered, the best is the one that makes the fewest assumptions.

In other words: Simple works best.

Like most people, I'm regularly tempted to tinker. So, if the original Couch Potato was a good thing, I thought, surely it can be improved with a little sophistication. Why not try some different asset classes? How about increasing the number of asset classes in the portfolio from 2 to 3?

Or 4, 5, 6, 7, 8, 9, or 10?

So I did it. The most complicated was called *the 10 Speed.*

Trust me, this is easy to do. Not long after introducing the original Couch Potato portfolio I introduced the Margarita portfolio. Regular readers of my column know that I am a fan of the other Buffett. That would be Jimmy Buffett, everything Parrothead, and Margaritaville. Like the drink, the Margarita portfolio is composed of three equal parts. But it is not made with tequila, triple sec, and fresh lime juice. It is made with equal parts domestic stocks, international stocks, and the total domestic bond market.

That, as you'll see in Chapter 14, is simple enough that it may be a reasonable solution to our investing problem.

But I wasn't satisfied with simplicity.

I went on to develop another seven portfolios. All had equal-sized investments (to make construction easy) in different asset classes. These asset classes included large-cap value, small-cap value, international value, emerging markets, real estate investment trusts (REITs), international bonds, and inflation-protected bonds.

Why those, you ask? I've got lots of excuses.

- Very credible research supported some investment in each asset class. Fama-French research, for instance, supports the idea of value investing – putting money into stocks that are selling at low multiples of book value and low price-to-earnings ratios. The same research also supports investing in small-cap stocks due to their capacity for unusual growth.

- Similarly, having a slug of real estate investment – usually in the form of REITs – has been found to increase returns while reducing risk. According to a Morningstar study, investors can benefit from an investment as small as 5 percent of a portfolio.

- International bonds are suggested as a hedge against too much dependence on the dollar. They often provide higher yields than domestic bonds.

- Emerging markets (EMs) are frequently recommended due to their superior demographics (rising population). EM equities also sell at a discount relative to more developed markets so they are value investments.

- Inflation-protected bonds are regular candidates because they are a way to guarantee a certain amount of purchasing power at a particular time. In addition, the real, after-inflation return on inflation-protected bonds has been far better than the return on traditional coupon bonds – *in some periods.*

THE CASE AGAINST DIVERSIFICATION

It all sounds so reasonable. What's the problem?

Well, there are two.

The first problem is complexity. The more elements you have, the more time you'll need to manage the portfolio. It also means more math exercises when it comes time to rebalance, even if you do it only once a year. You end up with 3, 5, 7, or 10 uneasy pieces.

Worse, you'll hear voices declaring that one asset class, or another, is a particularly good investment *right now*. Result? You've lost the serenity of being a Couch Potato investor.

The second problem is cyclicality. While value stocks, small stocks, international stocks, and emerging market stocks can provide higher returns (with higher risk) over very long periods of time, they can also trail the broad market index over periods of time longer than most investors have – or can bear.

The only thing you can be certain of, regardless of how you invest your money, is that there will be a time, perhaps many, when you doubt you've made the right choices. There will be a time like that for the Couch Potato portfolio, too.

Here's an example, using the analysis tools on www.portfoliovisualizer .com.

The worst decade for domestic stocks was the 2000s. From January 2000 through December 2009, the annualized return on US stocks was 0.95 percent. It was the lowest of all 10 asset classes used in my 10 Speed portfolio. REITs claimed the highest return at 10.40 percent annualized. Emerging markets followed at 9.82 percent, annualized.

Surely the basic 50/50 Couch Potato portfolio was a huge mistake. Right?

Wrong.

Over the decade, the Couch Potato trailed the 10 Speed portfolio with an annualized return of 6.32 percent, only 0.22 percent behind the 6.54 percent annualized return of the 10 Speed. Is the extra effort worth the additional return?

I don't think so.

But the case for simplicity doesn't end there. It turns out the additional return of the 10 Speed portfolio wasn't "free." You not only needed to expend more effort. You also had to take more risk. Over that decade the standard deviation (a measure of risk) of the 50/50 Couch Potato was 8.18 percent while the standard deviation of the 10 Speed was 10.36 percent – a hefty amount higher.

This slays a sacred cow of portfolio construction: that broad diversification reduces risk. Here, in the worst decade for the US stock market, diversification *added* risk. Table 13.1 compares the return and risk figures of four different portfolios. It reveals that the least complicated of the portfolios produced the best returns after adjustment for risk.

Table 13.1 Simplicity Won Out in the Oughts, When US Stocks Did Worst by Percentage.

Portfolio	Annualized Return	Standard Deviation	Modigliani-Modigliani (M2)*
CP 50/50	6.32	8.18	**10.86**
10 Speed	6.54	10.36	9.57
Margarita	6.03	10.71	8.65
60/40 Balanced	6.79	9.56	10.45

*See the next section for an explanation of this term; basically, it equalizes for risk.
Source: www.portfoliovisualizer.com.

DENZEL WASHINGTON ISN'T THE ONLY EQUALIZER

Many advisors, whether they work for a brokerage house or are registered investment advisors, like to tell clients research shows that different asset classes have higher long-term returns than the US stock market. That's quite true. The research for which Eugene Fama won a Nobel Prize in economics clearly shows that large-cap value stocks, small-cap stocks, and small-cap value stocks all offer higher long-term returns.

What the advisors forget to mention, despite Fama's clarity on the subject, is that increased returns are accompanied by increased risk.

As the saying goes: There is no free (investment) lunch.

Standard deviation is a metric that is used to indicate the variation in a sample. In the case of investment returns, it's an abstract number that gives us a sense of how much the price of a given asset class will vary. The more it varies, the greater the risk.

A more visceral metric is called Modigliani-Modigliani, often referenced as M2. This is not a reference to extremely slender sculpture pieces by artist and sculptor Amedeo Modigliani. M2 was created by Leah Modigliani, granddaughter of the MIT Nobel laureate Franco Modigliani. This metric compares portfolios by asking how much the return would be if you added enough riskless cash to equalize their risk.

As you can see from the figures in Table 13.1, the M2 of the basic Couch Potato portfolio tops the list. It even beats the traditional 60/40 equities/bonds "balanced" portfolio.

This leaves us with an observation and a question. The observation is well known: You don't get return without risk. You ignore risk at your peril.

The question is seldom asked: How much return are we willing to give up for a better shot at tranquility and good sleep?

For me the answer is easy: A small reduction in return is a small price to pay for good sleep, particularly when I'm confident that the long-term return will be enough to finance retirement.

That one word, *enough*, is crucial.

All too often, we abandon it in pursuit of "more." Indeed, it's so important that John C. Bogle wrote a book by that title: *Enough* (Wiley, 2010). It's a good read.

RELATED COLUMNS

Scott Burns, "Examining Your Gift Horse," 4/17/2001, https://scottburns.com/examining-your-gift-horse/

Scott Burns, "For Couch Potato Investors, 2012 Was a Good Year for Margaritas," 2/17/2013, https://scottburns.com/for-couch-potato-investors-2012-was-a-good-year-for-margaritas/

SOURCES AND REFERENCES

Jeremy Pagan, "The Rold of Real Estate Investments in a Portfolio," 1/11/2023, https://www.morningstar.com/funds/role-real-estate-investments-portfolio

Jimmy Buffett Singing "Margaritaville" on YouTube, https://www.youtube.com/watch?v=mrF4nF8VUb4

Modigliani-Modigliani as defined on Wikipedia, https://en.wikipedia.org/wiki/Modigliani_risk-adjusted_performance#:~:text=Modigliani%20risk%2Dadjusted%20performance%20(also,(e.g.%2C%20the%20market).

CHAPTER FOURTEEN

RIFFS ON THE COUCH POTATO PORTFOLIO TO CONSIDER

Index investing is an investment strategy that Walter Mitty would love. It takes very little investment knowledge, no skill, practically no time or effort – and outperforms about 80 percent of all investors. It allows you to spend your time working, playing, or doing anything else while your nest egg compounds on autopilot. It's about as difficult as breathing and about as time-consuming as going to a fast-food restaurant once a year.

—Taylor Larimore

Taylor Larimore started a website named the *Vanguard Diehards* in 1998. Its purpose was to be a place for people interested in index investing to gather, support each other, and answer questions.

That was 10 years after Bruce Willis starred in *Die Hard*, launching the sweet action and mayhem movie that millions of people watch every year at Christmas. It was also in the very early years of the World Wide Web, the original HTML code having been introduced in 1993.

But that was then.

Today, the site has been renamed *Bogleheads*, in honor of John C. Bogle, the founder of Vanguard and the father of low-cost index investing. The group also has a Facebook page. Beyond the media presence, the Bogleheads have grown to have dozens of US chapters, additional chapters in 9 countries, and an annual conference attended by hundreds.

THE THREE-FUND PORTFOLIO

Larimore introduced a three-fund portfolio in 2018 in his book, *The Bogleheads' Guide to the Three-Fund Portfolio: How a Simple Portfolio of Three Total Market Index Funds Outperforms Most Investors with Less Risk* (Wiley).

And it does. One study, cited in the book, compares the performance of the three-fund portfolio to the return of the average college endowment over periods from 1 to 10 years (see Table 14.1).

Table 14.1   The Three-Fund Portfolio Versus College Endowments by Percentage.

Endowments	1 Year	3 Years	5 Years	10 Years
The Three-Fund Portfolio	14.9	5.6	10.3	5.5
Average Endowment Return	12.2	4.2	7.9	4.5

Source: Larimore, *The Bogleheads' Guide to the Three-Fund Portfolio* (Wiley, 2018), 61.

It's useful to note here that college endowment funds have immense freedom and usually exercise it. In addition to individual stocks anywhere in the world, they can invest in real estate, hedge funds, timber, and derivatives of all kinds. The Texas Teachers' pension fund, for instance, has had a slug of precious metals investment for years.

The same funds are also known to pay high fees for the most sophisticated advice, a practice that very likely contributes to their failure to beat a simple three-fund portfolio.

Other research cited in the book shows that the probability of failing to beat a simple portfolio increases with both the number of funds in the portfolio and the period of investment. The research was done by Allan Roth, one of my favorite writers and a whiz at analysis. Table 14.2 compares the performance of an index fund portfolio with an active fund portfolio over periods of time and with different numbers of funds in the portfolio. The percentage of successful active portfolios declines as the number of funds increases *and* as the number of years increases.

Table 14.2   An Index Fund Portfolio Versus Actively Managed Fund Portfolios by Percentage.

Fund Count	1 Year	5 Years	10 Years	25 Years
1 Active Fund	42	30	23	12
5 Active Funds	32	18	11	3
10 Active Funds	25	9	6	1

Source: Larimore, *The Bogleheads' Guide to the Three-Fund Portfolio* (Wiley, 2018), 61.

This study assumed an average index fund annual cost of 0.23 percent – higher than current index fund costs – and 2.0 percent for the managed funds. While the failure rate will change as the difference in expenses changes, the reality is that managed funds are burdened with a wide variety of costs that the broadest index funds simply don't have. Regular evidence of this shows up every six months in the semiannual SPIVA reports comparing active fund returns, category by category, to their benchmark index.

WHAT'S IN THE THREE-FUND PORTFOLIO?

By now you're wondering what's in this three-fund portfolio. In his book Larimore cites three mutual funds:

- Vanguard Total Stock Market Index Fund (VTSMX)
- Vanguard Total Bond Market Index Fund (VBMFX)
- Vanguard Total International Stock Index Fund (VGTSX)

Today, you can use Vanguard's slightly lower cost and more tax-efficient exchange-traded funds:

- Vanguard Total Stock Market ETF (VTI)
- Vanguard Total Bond Market ETF (BND)
- Vanguard Total International Stock ETF (VXUS)

Yes, those are the exact three ingredients of the Margarita portfolio you saw in Chapter 13. Taylor Larimore, however, doesn't specify a precise allocation of the funds in his book.

So let's measure it at the equal allocation of the basic Couch Potato portfolio and see how it compares.

Table 14.3 shows what the data tells us when we compare portfolio performance over different time periods using www.portfoliovisualizer. It shows the standard deviation and Modigliani-Modigliani (M2) figures for each portfolio. (Remember that M2 compares portfolios by asking how much the return would be if you added enough riskless cash to equalize their risk). Note that the basic 50/50 Couch Potato portfolio provided less risk and, as a result, the highest risk-adjusted performance.

As you can see, the three-fund Margarita portfolio provided a higher return than the Couch Potato portfolio over the trailing three- and five-year periods. But it trailed over the last 10 years and for the longest possible measuring period, 1/87–3/25. It also had more risk. That resulted in a lower risk-adjusted return as measured by the Modigliani-Modigliani index, M2.

Table 14.3   Comparing Three Asset Class Portfolios.

Portfolio	3 Years	5 Years	10 Years	1/87–3/25	Std. Dev.	M2
60/40	5.2%	10.39%	7.67%	8.70%	12.97	12.31
Couch Potato	4.45	8.54	6.64	8.16	11.86	**12.65**
Margarita	4.49	9.31	6.15	7.53	12.96	10.20

NOTE: Bold numbers have the highest risk-adjusted return based on the M2 figure. They also have a materially lower standard deviation.
SOURCE: www.portfoliovisualizer.com

Meanwhile, the standard 60/40 balanced fund of domestic stocks and bonds beat the basic Couch Potato portfolio over 3-, 5- and 10-year periods as well as over the longest period, but it also had higher risk. It's risk-adjusted return is slightly lower than the Couch Potato portfolio.

Does that mean the Larimore's three-fund portfolio is down for the count?

For most people, most of the time, the answer is to let simplicity prevail.

One argument *for* the Margarita portfolio is the possibility of a broad, secular change – the idea that the hegemony of the United States – our status as the world's greatest power – is diminishing or even ending. As I write this, here are the strong arguments for this thought:

- The uncertainty of the aggressive tariff policies of the Trump administration
- The power of Chinese manufacturing and trade surplus
- The desire of the BRIC nations to eliminate the dollar as the world's reserve currency
- The divorce of US and European shared interests

If you think that argument will become history, then the Margarita portfolio is your security blanket. But you'll need to live with some increased risk.

If you have an immediate urge to make that decision, let me remind you of another factor. It will offset, to a substantial degree, the argument for international stocks in addition to domestic stocks.

Here's the other factor: You can't identify the revenue sources of a company by its home address. According to a study by S&P Global, for instance, 43.6 percent of sales by the S&P 500 companies were in foreign countries. Coca-Cola, a canonical American company, has 58.4 percent of its sales outside of the United States. The comparable figure for Walmart is 24.1 percent, 40.1 percent for Ford, and 58.1 percent for Procter & Gamble.

All those international sales by US companies are usually done in local currencies with local labor and equipment.

It goes the other way, too. The United States is the major revenue source for Toyota and Honda, quintessential Japanese companies. At the far extreme, Nestle only derives 3 percent of its revenue from its home country, Switzerland.

As they say, "It's complicated."

A RIFF THAT'S LIKELY TO WORK

In investing, there's nothing quite like certainty. The whole reason for diversification is to reduce risk and uncertainty. That's why bonds are included in most retiree portfolios. It's standard bank trust department practice. Ditto endowments, charitable foundations, and pensions.

Unfortunately, bonds have a problem. While a bond promises to return your original investment back at maturity and to pay interest until maturity, it only promises to pay back the nominal amount borrowed. It doesn't guarantee to return your original purchasing power.

Historically, the result has been painful. Interest has been received, but both the interest payments and the final return of principal will have lost purchasing power. From 1990 through 2024, for instance, the purchasing power of $100 declined to about $40 according to the U.S. Bureau of Labor Statistics CPI Inflation Calculator.

Retirees can avoid this by building "ladders" of Treasury Inflation-Protected Securities (TIPS) in their tax-deferred retirement accounts. The subject gets a lot of attention on the Bogleheads website. A ladder is a series of securities that mature, year by year, for as many years as you wish to extend the ladder.

It takes some time to set up, but the result is that you have provided exact amounts of purchasing power, year after year, once it is established. So whatever happens in the stock (or bond) markets, you'll know how much you'll have in real purchasing power to distribute.

In theory, you could guarantee your purchasing power from retirement to age 100. But that's a bit excessive. You can protect yourself from most perils by building a ladder of 5–10 years and replacing each maturing security with longest step security.

SHOULD YOU BUILD A LADDER?

This is a lot more than any Couch Potato investor should be called on to do, so you can ignore it if you like.

But if you are retired and inclined to add this bit of protection to your retirement you can get help online. In fact, iShares will help you build it with its ladder building tool and provide a pdf document with measures of return and calculated amounts to buy of their term exchange-traded funds (ETFs) for TIPS.

These term ETFs have an annual expense cost of 0.10 percent and mature late in each stated year. A bond for 2026, for instance, will mature in October 2026, in time for your annual required minimum distribution (RMD). This will provide you with cash for the following year, 2027. A bond for 2027 will mature in October 2027 and provide you with cash for your 2028 RMD.

RELATED COLUMNS

Scott Burns, "For Couch Potato Investors, 2012 Was a Good Year for Margaritas," 2/17/2013, https://scottburns.com/for-couch-potato-investors-2012-was-a-good-year-for-margaritas/

Scott Burns, "The Simplicity Manifesto," 3/31/2019, https://scottburns.com/the-simplicity-manifesto/

SOURCES AND REFERENCES

iShares ladder building tool, https://www.blackrock.com/us/financial-professionals/tools/ibonds

The U.S. Bureau of Labor Statistics CPI Inflation Calculator, https://www.bls.gov/data/inflation_calculator.htm

CHAPTER FIFTEEN

THE BONUS OF LOW-COST COMPOUNDING WHILE GROWING

Either we pay the government's bills, or we leave them for our kids to pay. It's that simple.

—Laurence J. Kotlikoff

E veryone knows that costs matter. Except in investing, of course. In that realm, high expenses are the juice that brings the high returns. It was ever thus.

No, I haven't gone crazy.

I just adopted the stance of the financial services industry for two sentences. Investment fees always matter. A huge body of evidence lets us know that we can benefit as Couch Potato investors.

How?

Easy. By taking advantage of the amazingly low costs of the biggest, lowest cost, exchange-traded funds.

HOW MUCH IS THAT IN DOLLARS?

But how much will we gain in dollars? Over decades of time?

That's a much more difficult question to answer.

Here's an example of the difference using a popular online calculator.

According to the Schwab Moneywise Investment Fee Calculator, here's what happens if a 25-year-old starts investing at age 25 and invests $6,000 a year for 37 years in a portfolio with an expense ratio of 0.04 percent a year and an 8 percent annual return:

- Over those 37 years $228,000 will be invested. It will grow to $1,360,340.
- Raise the costs to 1 percent a year and it will grow to $1,071,465 – $288,875 less.
- Raise the costs to 2 percent a year and it will grow to $840,022 – $520,319 less.

As a practical matter, this understates the cost because it assumes retirement at age 62. But if the 25-year-old works until age 65, when eligible for Medicare, the accumulation grows further. But so do the amounts lost to high fees:

- Over 40 years $246,000 invested will grow to $1,732,035.
- Raise costs to 1 percent a year and it will grow to $1,332,605 – $399,430 less.

- Raise costs to 2 percent a year and it will grow to $1,020,197 – $711,838 less.

These are illustration numbers, projections for an amazingly stable world where markets don't fluctuate, inflation isn't a consideration, and people never change jobs or see large shifts, up or down, in their income. (Send me the address, please!)

The important thing here is that the difference and accumulated assets by the time you retire can be measured in *years* of your final earned income. Exactly how many years will depend on the growth and stability of your income and the rate of inflation.

All these missing factors can be guessed at using the computing power accessible on today's mobile phones, not to mention a standard cheapo laptop. The only problem is that whatever computation tool you use, the answer will still depend on what you assume for work history, wage changes, market volatility, inflation, and eventual investment returns. That's a lot of assumptions.

BACK TO THE RAZOR!

It's a good reminder of Occam's razor – the answer with the least assumptions is likely to be the best one. In that case, the Schwab calculator tells you that the longer you pay less in fees, the greater your retirement savings will be – and the more likely you are to accumulate enough to retire in comfort.

Want more comfort?

Sorry, that requires assumptions.

Not happy with my answer? Don't worry. I won't judge you because it has never made me happy, either.

THE BEST AVAILABLE LONG-TERM PLANNING TOOL

The only tool I know of that allows you to make a broad series of assumptions about economic conditions and combine them with expected life events is a program developed by Lawrence J. Kotlikoff. He's a professor of economics at Boston University and, more important, one of the creators (with economist Alan Auerbach at UC Berkeley) of generational accounting. Most of his academic and consulting work deals with public policy issues. You can learn more about Kotlikoff on his Substack (https://larrykotlikoff.substack.com).

But his MAXIFI Planner is for real people – or at least their Certified Financial Planners. Available on the web, the program allows you to enter a plethora of data and assumptions and then calculates a stable lifetime income to age 100 based on those assumptions.

I admire Kotlikoff's work so much that I've coauthored three books with him, two for MIT Press (*The Coming Generational Storm: What You Need to Know About America's Economic Future*, 2004; *The Clash of Generations: Saving Ourselves, Our Kids, and Our Economy*, 2012) and one for Simon & Schuster (*Spend 'til the End: The Revolutionary Guide to Raising Your Living Standard – Today and When You Retire*, 2008). To be sure, I'm Boswell to his Dr. Johnson, but developing these books has been a fundamental growth and learning experience for me.

What will using MAXIFI Planner do for you?

It won't predict the future. Instead, it will let you explore, under a given set of assumptions, the decisions you can make that have the most leverage on your long-term standard of living.

The most interesting period, as you'll soon see, is the watershed years as you approach retirement and the decisions you make once retired.

RELATED COLUMNS

Scott Burns, "Living Standard Risk," 2/1/2007, https://scottburns.com/living-standard-risk/

Scott Burns, "Your Wealth Is Not Your Standard of Living," 3/1/2009, https://scottburns.com/your-wealth-is-not-your-standard-of-living-2/

Scott Burns, "The Thinness of Wealth," 5/24/2015, https://scottburns.com/the-thinness-of-wealth/

Scott Burns, "The Great Equalizers: Social Security and Pensions," 2/22/2016, https://scottburns.com/the-great-equalizers-social-security-and-pensions/

Scott Burns, "Money Magic Is Real Life Magic," 1/29/2022, https://scottburns.com/the-power-of-personal-decisions/

Scott Burns, "Talking (Really) Personal Finance," 1/22/2023, https://scottburns.com/youtube-podcast-interview/ (Me being interviewed on Kotlikoff's YouTube podcast)

SOURCES AND REFERENCES

MAXIFI Planner website, https://maxifiplanner.com

The Schwab Moneywise Compound Savings Calculator, https://www.schwabmoneywise.com/compound-savings-calculator

CHAPTER SIXTEEN

THE BONUS OF LOW-COST INVESTING WHILE SPENDING

"How did you go bankrupt?" Bill asked.
"Two ways," Mike said. "Gradually and then suddenly."
—Ernest Hemingway

W e've been hearing a lot about bankruptcy. As our economy becomes more stressed, the daily news is hardly complete without a bankruptcy story. And the bankruptcy always follows Hemingway's description. First, a few stories about difficulties. Then, suddenly, a filing for bankruptcy.

The same can happen to you and me in retirement: Suddenly, there is too much month at the end of the money. For the last 50 years the most common causes of personal bankruptcy have been the same. The three major causes are job loss, divorce, and medical expenses. Or any combination of the three.

In retirement there is another cause of bankruptcy – or sudden impoverishment – but it never makes it into the statistics.

THE INVISIBLE, BUT TERRIBLE, CAUSE OF LOSS

High investment management fees – whatever stands between you and the return on your savings is the invisible nest egg killer. The greater the fee burden, the greater the attrition of your retirement nest egg.

This reality is never recognized by the people in financial services. They will never understand why expenses reduce returns for a simple reason. *They can't afford to understand it.*

Let's explore exactly how investment expenses reduce your returns, your income, and your long-term security. We can do this with a Monte Carlo simulation tool available at www.portfoliovisualizer.

PLAYING RUSSIAN ROULETTE IN MONTE CARLO

Suppose you're about to retire. You've squirreled away a cool million in your 401(k) plan. You're thinking you'd like to live better now so you decide to have an initial 6 percent withdrawal rate from your investments. You'll adjust that $60,000 upward each year for inflation.

It's a practical idea: Life is short so eat dessert first. Taking 6 percent at the start increases your risk of running out of money late in retirement. Unfortunately, the investment fee also takes a toll, increasing the risk you'll run out of money.

But you'll start with money to travel! Maybe it will be worth the risk. If your portfolio value falls significantly, simple aging to lower spending may bail you out. Recall, in Chapter 4, we discussed "the retirement smile" – the idea that our spending declines as we age.

Total spending rises only when we are much older. That's when rising medical expenses overbalance what we're no longer spending in other areas.

The problem here is that investment expenses seriously increase the risk of running out of money. When you are distributing money to spend every year, the burden of withdrawals – including management fees – will be exaggerated in down markets, accelerating the decline of your savings. Table 16.1 shows the distribution of results by percentile of 50/50 Couch Potato portfolio with a starting value of $1 million and an initial withdrawal of $60,000 a year adjusted annually for inflation for management fee levels of 1 percent and 0.1 percent.

Table 16.1   Portfolio Survival Versus Investment Fees.

Fee Level (%)	10th Ptile Survival Years	25th Ptile Survival Years	50th Ptile Survival Years	75th Ptile Survival Years	Survival Rate (%)
0.1	20	26	30+	30+	64.5
1.0	18	21	29	30+	37.8

Source: www.portfoliovisualizer.com

As you can see, a relatively high starting withdrawal rate isn't a very good option, regardless of fee level. If you happen to retire in the bottom 10 percent of all probable futures, you'll be broke in 18 to 20 years. So if you retired at 62, the earliest you can collect Social Security, you'd be broke by your 80th to 82nd birthday. Overall, the low expense portfolio survives 64.5 percent of the time while the higher cost portfolio survives only 37.8 percent of the time.

THE EASY WAY OUT

Can you escape this fate?

If reader mail is any indication, the easy way out is to assume early death. Year after year readers tell me they're sure their money will last long enough because they'll be dead by age 73 or 75.

According to the life table used in the 2024 Annual Social Security Trustees Report, however, the remaining life expectancy of a male at age 62 is 19 years. It's 22 years for women of the same age. And life expectancy isn't a "dead by" date. It's the time when the average of a broad sample can be expected to have died.

The others – usually considered the lucky ones – will live longer. A few will become centenarians.

Unless you have a dismal family health history or intend to take up heavy smoking, drinking, and skydiving, the odds are against being dead by 75.

Sorry about that.

If you find this topic interesting – but not interesting enough to explore actuarial life tables – I suggest reading "The Lotus Eater" by W. Somerset Maugham. It's about a man who decides to buy an income annuity that stops at age 65 and goes to live on the island of Capri. At 65, he faces his intent to die when his income stops.

Big problem.

LIVING AND DYING
WITH THE ACTUARIES

If you find the topic of life and death intriguing, you need to meet Michael Kitces. While much of the research on retirement comes from academia, Kitces is a practitioner extraordinaire. He does research and broadcasts it to the field. One of the tools he created is an Excel model that enables you to input age and sex to explore survival percentages. The numbers that appear should discourage anyone who assumes an early death. Table 16.2 is a sample. Starting with a man and woman at age 65, it shows the probability of survival to different ages as single individuals, and as a couple. In couples the same age, women are generally about twice as likely to be the survivor.

Men have a 76 percent chance of still being alive at 75. For women, it's an 83 percent chance. If you've enjoyed a higher income than most and have a college education, the probabilities are still higher.

Table 16.2   The Probability of Still Being Here, By Age and Sex.

Age	He/She	Both	Neither	Either	He Only/She Only
65	100/100	100	0	100	0/0
75	76/83	63	4	96	13/20
80	58/69	40	13	87	18/29
85	37/51	19	31	69	18/32
90	18/29	5	58	42	12/24
95	5/11	1	84	16	5/11
100	1/2	0	97	3	1/2

SOURCE: https://www.kitces.com/?s=Life+expectancy+calculator&submit=&by-author=&by-category=&from-date=&to-date=

MAKING LIFETIME BETS FOR HIGHER SPENDING

But if you seek absolute certainty of not running out of money, you're likely to leave a lot of money behind.

The problem of lost spending opportunities intrigued Michael Finke enough that he decided it needed to be researched. Then at Texas Tech, he partnered with Wade Pfau and Duncan Williams to explore how much a couple could increase spending from their retirement portfolio by accepting the risk of running out of money. (Pfau and Finke are now at the American College for Financial Services and Williams has a financial planning firm.)

Here's a striking juxtaposition from their research. For a married couple taking a typical 4 percent from their portfolio, they could hold 30 to 60 percent in equities and be virtually assured of not outliving their retirement savings. At lower, or higher, equity allocations they faced a small chance of running out of money.

But if the withdrawal rate was doubled to 8 percent and their equity allocation was increased to a whopping 90 percent, they could *double* their spending at the price of spending 20 percent of their remaining life broke. For a 65-year-old couple with a joint life expectancy of 25 years, this translates into 20 years of having twice as much to spend, while facing 5 years of being broke starting at 85.

LEAVING THE GRIEVING WIDOW BROKE

The stark contrast here – double spending – will intrigue readers who are otherwise prudent. But, as the researchers pointed out, men have shorter lives than women. The real burden will most likely fall on a wife.

Does this mean we have to give up on any possibility of enjoying a spending rate higher than William Bengen's 4 percent safe withdrawal rate?

Very likely. But let's take a closer look at consumption smoothing and Bengen's 4 percent safe withdrawal rate rule. We may still have a way to take a higher spending rate, despite the risk.

CONSUMPTION SMOOTHING AND PORTFOLIO SURVIVAL

Economist Franco Modigliani won his Nobel Prize in economics for his work advancing the idea of "consumption smoothing" – the notion that we try to maintain an even level of consumption throughout our lives.

The idea of consumption smoothing was also behind the work of financial planner William Bengen when he tested portfolios to learn the safe withdrawal rate (SWR) – the spending level that could be adjusted for inflation each year and not run out of money for 30 years.

His first research found that a retiree could safely withdraw at an initial starting amount equal to 4.3 percent of the original portfolio. In subsequent work, he found ways to somewhat increase the SWR.

How consumption smoothing works depends very much on two things. First, it depends on the rate of inflation. Second, it depends on the return your portfolio earns in the first years of retirement. Retiring into a bear market is bad. Retiring into a bull market is good. Financial planners call this *sequence of returns risk.*

The combination of a bear market and high inflation in the 1970s, for instance, doomed the retirements of many who had retired in the late 1960s feeling rich.

For people who are overly optimistic, consumption smoothing can become a personal Wil E. Coyote experience – running confidently over a cliff – except it won't be funny.

ENTER PROMISE-BASED INCOME

Fortunately, everyone has a way to reduce the hazard of losing retirement savings. It's called Social Security. It's not investment-based income. It's promise-based income.

We all pay, directly and indirectly, a significant portion of our earned income to employment taxes. This entitles us to a promise-based retirement income that is inflation adjusted. For the 94 percent of all workers whose lifetime earnings are within the range of the annually adjusted wage-base maximum – $176,100 in 2025 – it's a very big deal.

Nor does promise-based income stop with Social Security.

While pensions are becoming rare, millions of workers still participate in corporate and public pension plans that promise a lifetime income. It's also possible to buy some promise-based income by purchasing a life annuity from an insurance company.

THE PROMISE-BASED INCOME SAFETY CUSHION

One of the most constructive exercises we can do is examine our spending and sort it into two categories: core and optional. Core spending is money we must spend to sustain what we consider to be our basic standard of living. That means the operating expenses of the house we own (hopefully mortgage free), the operating expenses of our automobiles, our out-of-pocket medical expenses, our communications and entertainment expenses, our spending on food and drink, and our spending on clothing.

Vacations, travel, new furnishings, and other things we can delay or cancel without much pain are the optional expenses.

If all your core expenses are covered by Social Security and other promise-based income, you would not be very vulnerable from running out of money with your asset-based retirement savings – whether it is in taxable accounts or tax-deferred accounts.

WHY THIS IS A PLEASANT SURPRISE FOR MOST PEOPLE

Advisors and the personal finance press tend to emphasize asset accumulation. When it comes to spending, they are out to lunch. Their advertising suggests we should spend more. Little or nothing is devoted to knowing how much we spend and where we spend it.

The people who pay attention to spending often find that much, or all, of their basic standard of living is covered by their promise-based income. This enables them to relax about the ups and downs of asset-based income from their retirement savings.

If you start paying attention, I think you'll be pleasantly surprised!

RELATED COLUMNS

Scott Burns, "Life: How Much Will You Leave on the Table?" 4/8/2012, https://scottburns.com/life-how-much-will-you-leave-on-the-table/

Scott Burns, "Live Long, Spend Freely," 3/20/2016, https://scottburns.com/live-long-spend-freely/

Scott Burns, "The Graceful, Soothing Curve of RMD Income," 6/19/2021, https://scottburns.com/curve-of-rmd-income/

Scott Burns, "Living Well, or Better, by Facing Death," 12/4/2021, https://scottburns.com/living-well-or-better-by-facing-death/

SOURCES AND REFERENCES

Michael Finke, Wade D. Pfau, and Duncan Williams, "Spending Flexibility and Safe Withdrawal Rates," *Journal of Financial Planning*, 2012, http://www.fpanet.org/journal/SpendingFlexibilityandSafeWithdrawalRates/

Michael Kitces, Life Expectancy Calculator, https://www.kitces.com/?s=Life+expectancy+calculator&submit=&by-author=&by-category=&from-date=&to-date=

W. Somerset Maugham, "The Lotus Eater," https://facultyweb.wcjc.edu/users/jonl/documents/LotusEater.pdf

Wei Sun and Anthony Webb, "Can Retirees Base Wealth Withdrawals on The IRS' Required Minimum Distributions?" Center for Retirement Research at Boston College, no 12–19, October 2012, https://crr.bc.edu/wp-content/uploads/2012/10/IB_12-19-508.pdf

CHAPTER SEVENTEEN

CAN YOU SPEND MORE?

It is better to spend money like there's no tomorrow than to spend tonight like there's no money.

—P. J. O'Rourke

Most of personal finance literature has a single goal: coaching us in saving and investing so that we'll have enough money that we can afford to retire and not run out of money.

It's a noble cause.

It's also necessary. Most people will fail miserably without some guidance. Even the many methods for increasing retirement spending start from the premise that we want to spend more but don't want to risk ruin.

But another group also needs help.

REHAB
FOR NON-SPENDERS

They are the non-spenders. The people who are so adept at saving and not spending that they keep accumulating money in retirement. They just can't spend money.

If you're in this group, read on. This chapter is for you.

One of the odd realities in the distribution of lifetime net worth is that it tends to continue rising even after we retire. I learned this years ago while assembling data for my "Wealth Scoreboard" columns. The columns used data from the Federal Reserve's "Survey of Consumer Finances," which is done every three years, to show the net worth of households at different ages and at different levels of wealth from the median net worth up to the top 1 percent. Table 17.1 shows, in thousands of dollars, the threshold net worth for a household to be at various levels of wealth at different ages. The amount includes all measurable sources of wealth, including home equity, which is a major portion of net worth at lower levels of net worth. It does not include what some call *virtual wealth* from guaranteed income such as Social Security and public and private pensions.

As you can see from Table 17.1, net worth doesn't top out in the peak earning years before retirement. It peaks in the 60s for those in the top 1 percent to top 25 percent. It peaks years later, age 70–74, for households at the median level. The assumption most economists make, particularly those with a life cycle frame of mind, is that we reach a level of security with our wealth. Then we decide we can risk spending or giving away assets.

Unless it's just too painful.

That raises the old saying: "If you don't fly first-class while you're alive, you can be sure your grandchildren will when you're dead." Feel free to makes substitutions for the first-class airfare. Think: second home, round-the-world cruise, belated orthodontistry, more single-malt Scotch,

Table 17.1   The American Wealth Scoreboard, 2022.

Age Group	Top 1%	Top 5%	Top 10%	Top 25%	Median
80+	$16,230	$5,461	$2,540	$944	$327
75–79	$19,869	$5,845	$2,914	$992	$338
70–74	$18,762	$6,198	$2,999	$1,235	**$439**
65–69	**$22,103**	**$6,865**	$2,961	**$1,155**	$393
60–64	$17,870	$6,366	**$3,042**	$1,131	$393
55–59	$15,372	$6,050	$2,672	$1,137	$321
50–54	$13,232	$4,419	$2,577	$913	$266
45–49	$8,701	$2,790	$1,429	$680	$214
40–44	$7,835	$1,971	$1,183	$437	$134
35–39	$4,741	$1,482	$864	$389	$139
30–34	$2,637	$796	$539	$186	$89
25–29	$2,122	$410	$297	$131	$31
18–24	$653	$422	$185	$34	$10

NOTE: The figures in bold type are the level at which net worth peaks, an indication that wealthy people start to distribute their wealth in their 60s.
SOURCES: Federal Reserve Survey of Consumer Finances, https://dqydj.com/net-worth/, published previously in "The Post-Covid Wealth Scoreboard," https://scottburns.com/the-post-covid-wealth-scoreboard/

unrelenting plastic surgery, whatever . . . . This can get banal very fast. But it's your money. You can do anything you please with it.

If you dare.

You can also have more altruistic and generative ideas. Some couples will need to confront the reality that their children may inherit money rather late in life. A child born when you are 25, for instance, will inherit at 70 if you die at 95. This suggests gifting earlier may be far more meaningful than inheriting later.

The same applies to charitable giving. The earlier you give, the more time you will have to enjoy knowing that your gift benefited real, living people in the here and now.

IS THERE A TOOL FOR SAFELY ESTIMATING HOW MUCH YOU CAN SPEND?

The big question the non-spenders face is how do they *safely* spend more? There are plenty of relatively complicated methods to increase retirement spending. Indeed, there is a vast literature of methods.

But is there a simple tool?

The answer is yes. It came from M. Barton Waring and Laurence B. Segal in 2015. In a paper for the *Financial Analysts Journal*, they declared that retirement spending was essentially an annuitization problem. You would be safe (never running out of money), if you calculated an annuity rate every year and never spent more.

ARVA: ANNUALLY RECALCULATED VIRTUAL ANNUITY

Basically, they were going beyond any "safe withdrawal rate" rules and establishing a maximum you could spend and never run out of money because you were recalculating your maximum spending based on your life expectancy each year.

It wasn't even necessary to buy an annuity! You only needed to calculate the spend amount each year. Then spend that amount and repeat the process the following year, based on your new life expectancy and remaining financial assets. You'd never run out of money, but your annual maximum spending will vary with changes in the value of your investments.

The math and theory in all this are well beyond simple, so let's find a way this idea can help retirees who would like to find out how much they can spend without registering for graduate school.

You Are Single and Have Retired Early at Age 62

You want to know a safe spend rate. Where will you get it? Not from the IRS. Under the most recent rules, there is no required minimum withdrawal until age 73 for those born from 1951 through 1959 and 75 for those born in 1960 or later. When they do give you a number, it's wildly conservative at 27.4 years. This represents the *joint* life expectancy of a couple where the younger is 10 years younger than the person taking the required minimum distribution (RMD).

Got that?

The IRS is telling you to assume that your "uniform" life expectancy is 72 + 27.4 or 99.4 years. In fact, only about 1 percent of males can be expected to live to that age.

While it is better that the assumptions of life expectancy for retirement account withdrawals are conservative so that fewer people will run out of money under government direction, our personal decisions could be made on a more realistic basis.

Life expectancy for males at age 62 is 21.7 years. For women it's a bit under 24.5 years. This suggests an ARVA withdrawal rate of between 4 and 5 percent. It also suggests that Bengen's 4-plus percent safe withdrawal rate is a broadly useful guide.

You Are Single, Own Your Home Debt-Free and Are Age 80

Social Security covers most, or all, of what you spend because you've been cautious for years of retirement. You're also learning that you're likely to leave a lot of money behind. With 80-year-old life expectancy at 8.9 years for men and 10.3 years for women, this suggests an ARVA of about 10 percent. This is about *double* the 5 percent rate suggested by the IRS uniform lifetime table for minimum required distributions.

In Table 17.2 I show calculated ARVAs from age 72 to age 85 based on Social Security life expectancies at each age. It compares RMD rates from

Table 17.2 Required Minimum Distributions Versus Actual Life Expectancy-Based Rates.

Age	Uniform Life Table (%)	Male Life Expectancy ARVA (%)	Female Life Expectancy ARVA (%)
72	3.65%	7.05	6.21
73	3.77	7.46	6.54
74	3.99	7.87	6.90
75	4.06	8.33	7.25
76	4.22	8.77	7.69
77	4.37	9.35	8.20
78	4.54	9.90	8.62
79	4.74	10.53	9.17
80	4.95	11.24	9.71
81	5.16	12.05	10.42
82	5.40	12.82	11.11
83	5.65	13.70	11.90
84	5.95	14.70	12.66
85	6.25	15.87	13.51

SOURCES: Adapted from Social Security Life Expectancy Calculator, https://www.ssa.gov/OACT/population/longevity. html; IRS Uniform Lifetime Table, https://www.irs.gov/publications/p590b#en_US_2024_publink100090310

age 72 to 85 showing a large spending difference provided the individuals basic income and shelter are secure. The advantage for married couples is smaller due to joint life expectancy rather than single life expectancy. As you can see, the conservative basis of the Uniform Lifetime table suggests a much lower annual distribution and spending rate than the ARVAs.

If your basic living expenses are covered by Social Security, or Social Security and promise-based assets, and you are at ease with your shelter situation, you can safely increase the amount you withdraw and spend from your financial assets up to the amount suggested by the table.

Sorry, you'll still need to find the courage to spend.

RELATED COLUMNS

Scott Burns, "Life: How Much Will You Leave on The Table?," 4/8/2012, https://scottburns.com/life-how-much-will-you-leave-on-the-table/

Scott Burns, "Score Yourself for Wealth," 6/4/2000, https://scottburns.com/score-yourself-for-wealth/

Scott Burns, "Living Well, Or Better, By Facing Death," 12/4/2021, https://scottburns.com/living-well-or-better-by-facing-death/

Scott Burns, "The Post-Covid Wealth Scoreboard," 11/20/23, https://scottburns.com/the-post-covid-wealth-scoreboard/

SOURCE AND REFERENCE

M. Barton Waring, "The Only Spending Rule You'll Ever Need," 7/2014. https://larrysiegeldotorg.wordpress.com/wp-content/uploads/2014/09/siegel_waring_only-spending-rule-article-youll-ever-need.pdf

PART IV

THE PROOF IS IN THE PUDDING

CHAPTER EIGHTEEN

THE PUDDING REPORTS: IT'S ALL ABOUT THE CASH

Twenty years from now you will be more disappointed by the things you didn't do than by the ones you did do.

—Mark Twain

For most of us, the most important financial statistic isn't our rate of return or any of the obscure measurements used in the investment business. No, we go straight to the bottom line.

- How much is that in *dollars*?
- How much money do we have today compared to last year?
- Does it look like enough?

That's what it's all about. Does it look as though we've got enough money to do the things we hope to do in the time we have left? If the number says yes, we feel good. If the number says no, we feel bad.

THE PUDDING REPORTS

That's also why I started doing "The Pudding Report" years ago. I wanted to show readers how much money they would have left at the end of different retirement periods.

The news for the year-end of 2024 was pretty good. In fact, the news has been good every year I've done the report. I have, however, added an occasional note of angst for those who had retired into a major market swoon like 1999–2002.

Consider Table 18.1, taken from a column published in early 2025. If you had retired 30 years earlier, at age 65, you'd have enjoyed an inflation-adjusted income based on the original Bengen figure of 4.3 percent. So, you'd have started with $4,300 from a $100,000 nest egg. (Multiply by 10× to find the withdrawal amount for a $1 million nest egg.)

Table 18.1 Couch Potato Portfolio Ending Values After Distributions.

Time Period	End Value	Net Return (%)	Negative Years (number of years: year)	Worst Year Loss (%)
3 years	$117,337	5.47	1: 2018	−2.66
5 years	$131,677	5.66	1: 2018	−2.66
10 years	$159,991	4.81	1: 2018	−2.66
15 years	$156,925	3.05	2: 2008, 2018	−15.99
20 years	$127,946	1.24	4: 2001, 2002, 2008, 2018	−15.99
25 years	$271,272	4.07	4: 2001, 2002, 2008, 2018	−15.99
30 years	$569,683	5.97	5: 1994, 2001, 2002, 2008, 2018	−15.99

SOURCE: www.portfoliovisualizer.com

You'd have adjusted your income each year for inflation, including the post-COVID years. Your original $100,000 would now be $569,683. You'd also now be 95 years old.

BUT ARE YOU STILL ALIVE?

If you are still alive, which isn't too likely.

Remember, in Chapter 17, we learned the probability of a man still being alive at 95 from age 65. It was only 5 percent for men, 11 percent for women. If you had survived the period, you had been through four years of losing money. The worst year was a 16 percent loss.

Even if you had retired straight into the internet bust of 2001 and 2002, your $100,000 would have become $127,946. And at age 85 Mr. Kitces's table tells us that only 37 percent of men would have survived and 51 percent of women.

A retired couple has a 31 percent chance that both have died in 20 years. There is a 61 percent chance that only one of the couple is still alive. So the remaining money only needs to support one person instead of two. The odds for sustaining the survivor improve.

Earlier reports provide minor variations on the same theme – a simple, low-cost Couch Potato portfolio can provide a reliable, inflation-adjusted income for decades of retirement living.

Will this always be so reassuring? I can't say for certain. Neither can anyone else. But Bill Bengen's original work covered a century of massive change and upheaval. We suffered soaring inflation, not to mention unrelenting deflation and massive unemployment in the Great Depression. Or the stress of World War II. And don't forget decades of proxy wars fought all around the planet. All that upheaval – particularly inflation – and his work shows that a 4+ percent withdrawal rate survives the worst of times.

A simple Couch Potato portfolio would have financed a comfortable retirement. All you had to do was save enough, for a long enough period. No magic required. Only initiative. And persistence.

A MINOR LIMITATION

These figures have a limitation. They are based on asset class returns, not actual fund returns. So, they are a bit like the world physicists like to conjure: "assume a motor with no friction." Those who retired in 1985 or 1990 saw somewhat less success because they didn't have lower-cost investment choices. Vanguard introduced its Total Bond Market index mutual fund in 1986. The Total Stock Market mutual fund wasn't introduced until 1992. Although they existed from these dates doesn't mean that they were widely available to most investors except in taxable accounts.

BUT THIS IS NOW

But today, young workers starting out can be Couch Potato investors for their entire working life. This means they can invest in the lowest cost exchange-traded funds (ETFs) in their taxable account and in IRA accounts. Many corporate 401(k) plans still don't offer these lowest cost options as part of their plans. But the same plan may offer a "brokerage window" option that will provide access to the lowest cost ETFs.

Other corporate workers may work at companies that have followed the example of ExxonMobil and Texas Instruments. Both have long offered very low-cost index fund options in their employee plans. For decades. And if you are a federal employee, you already know that the Thrift Savings Plan offers fund selections perfect for the Couch Potato portfolio.

As a result, many young workers will have a lifetime low-cost investing bonus. Older workers may have lost money to unnecessary fees during their careers. But young workers may enter retirement with more in their nest eggs.

How much more? That's a tough question. It has enough variables to make any answer no more than a guess. So, here's a ballpark guesstimate. The difference in lifetime accumulation for investing 10 percent of annual gross income is about two or three *years* of final income. This means future retirees may start their retirements with 5–10 percent more income.

Important note: The 10 percent of starting income figure can be direct from salary. It can also be from a 6+ percent commitment for a worker with a 50 percent employer match. This estimate assumes that wages rise at the long-term rate of inflation, about 3 percent, which is rare for periods of 35 and 40 years. It also assumes that the contribution is fixed at the original amount. Finally, it makes no allowance for the ups and downs of markets, which create opportunities to buy more shares when markets are down and less when markets are up. That's why it's a ballpark figure.

RELATED COLUMN

Collection of "Pudding Report" columns, https://scottburns.com/?s=Pudding

SOURCES AND REFERENCES

Calculator for estimating future income/future value, https://www.calculator soup.com/calculators/financial/future-value-calculator.php

Michael Kitces's life expectancy calculator, https://www.kitces.com/?s=Life+ expectancy+calculator&submit=&by-author=&by-category=&from-date=& to-date=

Schwab investment fee comparison calculator, https://www.schwabmoneywise. com/investment-fees-calculator

PART V

THE REWARDS OF SIMPLICITY FOR ACTUAL PEOPLE

CHAPTER NINETEEN

HOW AVERAGE BECOMES SUPERIOR

Perfect is the enemy of good.

—Voltaire

Occam's razor tells us that the simple solution is usually the best. Voltaire's rule tells us that holding out for perfection stands in the way of doing something well.

Both are important notions for investors. They are particularly significant for those who value other aspects of life, like their time and sanity.

Here's a story to illustrate.

Many years ago, a stockbroker dismissed my interest in index funds as silly. "Who would settle for just average returns," he asked?

I bit my tongue. Providing a serious answer to his question was pointless. The broker, like most people who aren't engineers or social scientists, clearly didn't know statistics. Nor had he considered the implications of what he had said. He was a willing victim of his sales training.

Let's explore the implications. Then we'll examine the word *average*.

POWERFUL IMPLICATIONS

We invest money today so we can have money tomorrow to provide us with the things we need in the future. We do that because we know there will be a time when we can no longer earn money with our labor. Whether the return on our money is average, above average, or below average is irrelevant if the return is *enough* to fulfill our goals.

The only benefit of a higher-than-average return is that it opens the possibility of being able to spend more today since we'll need to save less to have *enough*.

If we need to have a superior, above average, return to meet our goals, we are increasing the odds that we will fail to reach our basic goal.

That may be necessary for some, but it's a bad idea. Why take a big chance on something as important as retirement?

Besides, who said we must compete in every aspect of our lives? It's quite enough, for most people, to deal with the need to compete in our chosen line of work. If you want to focus on making the best pizza in your area – or any other task – why should you have to try to win at investing, too?

POWERFUL STATISTICS

You've probably heard the joke about Bill Gates. It goes, "Bill Gates walks into a bar and the average income soars to $50 million from, maybe, $60,000."

While most jokes are told to get a laugh, this joke is told to illustrate the limitations of using averages.

All the people in the bar will have the same income after Gates enters as before. And the typical income in the bar – the median – will be unchanged as well. This illustrates that a single large data item can lead to a distorted view of the people in the bar.

Or anywhere else.

It is more useful to study *distributions* than to calculate averages for a sample. Research tells us that most money managers can't beat a broad index. It also tells us the following:

- Some managers will beat a broad index over a short time but very few will beat it over a long time.
- The longer the time, the lower the chances of beating the index.
- The more the manager charges, the lower the chances of beating the index over any time.
- A superior performance is usually the result of luck, not skill.

The net result is that if you think of the managers and their index as horses in a race, the best horse to bet on is the index. Why? Because it gives you the best odds of "winning" – coming out ahead of all the other horses.

Are you guaranteed to win?

Sorry, no. You always have a shot at betting on a managed horse that wins for a while. But, as you saw in Chapter 12, the longer the race, the better the odds the index will win. The most recent SPIVA report showed that broad domestic index beat 93.4 percent of all broad domestic equity funds just 15 years after the period started. A broad bond index beat 90.1 percent of all general domestic bond funds 15 years after the period started.

That brings us to a tough reality. Our time is heroically long. We invest during 35, or more, years of working. Then we continue investing for what may be another 35 years of retirement. That 70-plus years is about 10 times as long as the typical portfolio manager oversees a fund before moving on to another, according to industry statistics.

So, when it comes to investing, before and after retirement, what choice would you make knowing you've got a 90 percent chance of winning with a broad, tax-efficient index fund or a 10 percent chance of winning with a managed fund?

And that's just the money. The nonmoney benefits of Couch Potato investing are seldom discussed. But they are huge.

RELATED COLUMN

Scott Burns columns using SPIVA data, https://scottburns.com/?s=SPIVA

SOURCE AND REFERENCE

SPIVA Report, 2024, https://www.spglobal.com/spdji/en/documents/spiva/spiva-us-year-end-2024.pdf

CHAPTER TWENTY

THE UNSPOKEN FORMS OF CAPITAL

Our comforting conviction that the world makes sense rests on a secure foundation: our almost unlimited ability to ignore our ignorance.

—Daniel Kahneman, Thinking, Fast and Slow

"The streetlight effect" has fascinated me for half a century. Its history traces to a thirteenth-century Sufi story, but it applies to all searches. It affects all knowledge.

The fact that most economists build their ideas on a foundation of money statistics was so frustrating to me that I devoted my second book, published in 1975, to estimating the size, value, and potential of the household economy. That's all the work we do in our homes and communities that is not blessed by the payment of dollars. If it isn't measured, it is ignored.

The Streetlight Effect
Source: https://sketchplanations.com/looking-under-the-lamppost

We've come a long way since then. But the streetlight effect still dominates our perception. It obscures our understanding of true wealth. It makes a mess of our pursuit of financial freedom and independence.

THE FIVE FORMS OF WEALTH

The most recent book to shed light on the subject is Sahil Bloom's *The 5 Types of Wealth* (Ballantine Books, 2025). But it is just that: the most recent.

Rather than focus on financial wealth alone Bloom identifies five types of wealth:

- Time
- Social
- Mental
- Physical
- Financial

The only way for us to have full, productive, and happy lives, he argues, is to pay attention to all five forms of wealth. And he starts with time wealth. More accurately, he starts with how most of us suffer from time poverty. Bloom believes we suffer because we lead overscheduled, over-busy, overcommitted, and overworked lives.

He isn't the first.

The most practical book on the subject is *Your Money or Your Life* by Vicki Robin and Joe Dominguez (Penguin Books, 2018). First published in 1992, it is the cornerstone book for the Financial Independence, Retire Early movement. It lays out exactly how we exchange our time for money and how to change the balance.

TIME POVERTY

Juliet B. Schor, a professor at Boston College, has studied every aspect of our time poverty. See *The Overworked American: The Unexpected Decline of Leisure* (Basic Books, 1992) and *The Overspent American: Why We Want What We Don't Need* (Harper Perennial, 1999).

She also wrote a more positive book, *True Wealth: How and Why Millions of Americans Are Creating a Time-Rich, Ecologically Light, Small Scale, High Satisfaction Economy* (Penguin Books, 2011).

Dozens of books have been written about time, work, money, and leisure over the past half century. You could read some, but my bet is that most readers are already members of the choir.

So where does Couch Potato investing fit in? Easy.

Couch Potato investing is a step toward time freedom. It is the easiest thing you can do to recover all the time lost to watching talking heads, staring at monthly statements, doomscrolling financial gurus, or reading tomes about markets and investments. As a Couch Potato investor you can be assured that your savings have a high probability of doing better, perhaps far better, than the people who spend hours on nights and weekends trying to figure out what to do in the next few days, only to change their minds a week later.

GAINING TIME

Repurpose that wasted time, and you are on the path to gains in the other four forms of wealth: time, social, mental, and physical. Living in a money-obsessed society, we seldom have time to think about the possible benefits of changing our time commitments.

But here's a powerful example that Bloom provides in *The 5 Types of Wealth* (p. 4).

Friend	How often do you see your parents?
Me	Maybe once a year right now.
Friend	And how old are they?
Me	Mid-sixties.
Friend	Okay, so you're going to see your parents fifteen more times before they die.

A similar discussion applies to the amount of time we have to spend with our children. We become secondary in their lives about age 15, and they are running with their own agenda by age 18. Inevitably, we become less important in their lives. So, if your children are under 15, today – not tomorrow – is the day to find time for them.

Just as no one on their deathbed has ever said, "I should have spent more time at the office," no one has ever said, "I spent much too much time with my children."

RELATED COLUMNS

Scott Burns, "The Business of Debt Reduction," 12/21/1997, https://scott burns.com/the-business-of-debt-reduction/

Scott Burns, "Will You Ever Have Enough Money?" 5/31/1998, https://scott burns.com/will-you-ever-have-enough-money/

Scott Burns, "Whatever Happened to Leisure?," 7/12/2019, https://scottburns.com/whatever-happened-to-leisure/

Scott Burns, "Is Financial Independence Possible?," 9/28/2019, https://scott burns.com/is-financial-independence-possible/

Scott Burns, "Rearranging Life and Our Economy," 9/25/2022, https://scott burns.com/rearranging-life-and-our-economy/

SOURCE AND REFERENCE

Burns, S. (1975). *Home, Inc.: The Hidden Wealth and Power of the American Household*. Doubleday.

CHAPTER TWENTY-ONE

RISING ABOVE SERFDOM IN AN AGE OF NEO-FEUDALISM

I owe, I owe, so it's off to work I go.
—A popular revision of the song sung by the seven
dwarves in Disney's *Snow White*

Are you a serf?

Don't answer quickly. You may be one and not realize it.

In agrarian feudal society, serfs were at the bottom. They were tied to the land of their lord. Peasants had greater freedom. They were free to move from one area to another and often had valuable skills.

Today corporations have replaced the fiefdoms of yore. The big dogs at the top of those corporations have the power of lords, if not kings. An exploration of the dilemma faced by Elizabeth Bennet in Jane Austen's novel, *Pride and Prejudice*, can tell us a lot. According to Branko Milanovic in his wonderful book, *The Haves and the Have Nots: A Brief and Idiosyncratic History of Global Inequality* (Basic Book, 2011), Elizabeth Bennet was well-off by the standards of the day. Her families' independent income of 3,000 pounds a year put them in the top 1 percent of English society.

KEEPING ELIZABETH BENNETT

The Bennetts enjoyed living in a substantial country house and had servants to take care of daily needs and chores. They never faced the indignity of work. But their shelter was precarious since it would be gone at the death of Elizabeth's father. So would the family income. Elizabeth's share of her mother's dowry, if she had it, would be about 1,000 pounds. Milanovic estimates that it would have earned about 4 percent at the time, enough to produce an income of 40 pounds a year.

That was still a good sum. It was about twice the average income in England at the time. Most people would still be looking enviously at her circumstances.

But Mr. Darcy, her suitor, had an independent income of 10,000 pounds a year, more than three times her father's income. Darcy's income put him in the top one-tenth of 1 percent. More important, his income was equivalent to the income of 500 typical citizens at the time and 250 times what Elizabeth would have had to live on.

THE NEW LORDS OF THE LAND

Today, income is more equally distributed in England so the gap between Elizabeth and Darcy wouldn't be quite so compelling. But the big dogs today are no longer people living on inherited wealth. They are the folks at the top of major corporations.

While Henry the VIII was well clothed, well-housed, and had the power of life or death, Cromwell worked hard to keep him out of continental wars because Henry would have had trouble sustaining an army of any size. Jeff Bezos at Amazon, however, employs over 1.5 million people.

To put the army of Amazon workers in some perspective, only China has a larger army (2.18 million). India, with the second largest army in the world at 1.45 million is about equal to Amazon. The next three nations – the United States, Russia, and North Korea – have about 1.3 million in their armies.

THE KINGDOMS OF MUSK

Elon Musk, who works as assiduously (but more successfully) as Henry VIII to provide a legacy to the gene pool, employs 121,000 at Tesla, with more employees at his other companies. Indeed, the 50 largest US corporations have at least 100,000 employees each.

Big dog power exerts itself in many ways. My first personal glimpse of it occurred decades ago while visiting Don Kendall, the chairman of Pepsi-Cola, for a magazine article interview. His office, the size of a small house but lined with sound-deadening glass on two walls, overlooked a large park with a manufactured lake. The lake had a fountain in its center. It was not flowing when I first saw it.

I asked Kendall when the fountain flowed.

He smiled. He pushed a button under his desk with his knee, and the fountain erupted.

A few minutes later, Billy Graham called. A helicopter flew close by.

In complete silence.

HOW EMPLOYEES BECOME CORPORATE SERFS

It's easy to become a serf. Here are a few causes:

- Having too much personal debt to chance a job change; education debt looms large here, not just willy-nilly consumer debt
- Having a preexisting medical condition that might not be covered if they lost their employer-provided health insurance
- Being tied into a pension plan, or stock options, not yet vested

Whatever the reason, it is more subtle than the absolute power of a medieval lord. But it is just as limiting.

Neo-feudalism, a topic with a growing literature, is (yet) another school of dystopian thought. You can worry about it if you want.

But I'd rather take a happier route that is more productive.

Let's talk about steps you can take to maximize your personal freedom whether you take a conventional or neo-feudalist view.

TURNING THE LAFFER CURVE INTO AN UMBRELLA

Economist Arthur B. Laffer, who rose to public fame using a simple sketch on a napkin, was a member of President Reagan's Economic Policy Advisory Board. His sketch showed a high-peaked arc plotting tax revenue against tax rate. Revenue was on the vertical axis; tax rate was on the horizontal axis.

As the diagram showed, tax revenue first rises as the tax rate rises. But at some rate it peaks. Further increases in tax rates produce the opposite effect – tax revenues fall. Laffer argued that our taxes were too high. Lowering tax rates, he said, would increase tax revenue.

Whether it worked that way, in practice, is still being argued. In fact, it doesn't matter. What's important, is that the Laffer curve is really an umbrella that encourages us to do things for ourselves, our family, and our community. This umbrella also provides cover in retirement because we can still do things that are substitutes for earned (and taxed!) income. We can also make investments whose returns are in services (shelter, solar power, etc.) rather than taxable cash.

MEASURING THE SIZE OF THE LAFFER CURVE UMBRELLA IN THE GIG ECONOMY

According to Velocity Global, a human resource management firm, gig workers are sole proprietors and independent contractors who work short-term jobs in fields as diverse as Uber driving and computer coding. Most work remotely. Some 59 million workers – 36 percent of our workforce – do gigs, and 56 percent do gigs in addition to their regular work. Many others, like home handy workers, small contractors, and other self-employed people, also work by the gig, even if they don't consider themselves part of the gig economy.

The umbrella over this work is our Byzantine, multipart, tax system. Here are the tax rates an independent worker can face:

- 15.3 percent goes to paying the employment tax
- 10 percent to 22 percent federal income tax for single workers with incomes from $0 to $103,350
- 15 percent for loss of subsidy for Affordable Care Act health insurance for workers with incomes over the Medicaid limit

In effect, an independent worker – our fastest growing worker group – faces a marginal tax rate of about 40.3 percent as her income rises above poverty level. This is higher than the 37 percent marginal tax rate in the federal income tax for workers with income over $626,350.

Losing 40 percent of what you earn is a good reason to limit paid income and learn how to do as much as possible for yourself. It's a good reason to become a lifetime student at YouTube university, watching videos on how to do virtually any task imaginable.

Here's an example. Suppose you work as an on-call contract worker at several food trucks, and you are paid $20 an hour. The after-tax and health insurance net from this could be as low as $12 an hour.

Here's the alternative.

Having an electrician come to your house to repair or replace a blown circuit breaker or damaged outlet might cost you $150. So, watching a YouTube video to learn how to make the repair is worth $150 in after-tax cash. That's equivalent to 12.5 hours of work which is probably two days of shift work.

Lifetime learning pays!

The most profitable learning is the most practical, hands-on kind, like putting things together, fixing toilets, knowing how to unplug a disposal, and being able to sand, paint, or varnish.

We'll explore what I call the *un-money economy* in the next few chapters.

RELATED COLUMNS

Scott Burns, "Living the Good Life, Along with Riley," 9/7/2019, https://scott burns.com/living-the-good-life-along-with-riley/

Scott Burns, "Making a Plan to Retire Now, Not Later," 4/25/22, https://scott burns.com/working-out-the-moves-for-retiring-asap/

Scott Burns, "How to Join the Un-Money Economy and Prosper," 6/23/24, https:// scottburns.com/how-to-join-the-un-money-economy-and-prosper/

SOURCES AND REFERENCES

Google search for "neo-feudalism," https://www.google.com/search?client=safari &rls=en&q=Neo+feudalism&ie=UTF-8&oe=UTF-8

Investor.gov investment growth calculator, https://www.investor.gov/financial-tools-calculators/calculators/compound-interest-calculator

Kotkin, J. (2020). *The Coming of Neo-Feudalism: A Warning to the Global Middle Class*. Encounter Books.

MIT Living Wage Calculator, https://livingwage.mit.edu

Social Security Administration, Distribution of Social Security benefits by age and sex, https://www.ssa.gov/oact/progdata/benefits/ra_mbc202412.html

Velocity Global, Gig Economy statistics, https://velocityglobal.com/resources/blog/gig-economy-statistics/

Website for the Foundation for Intentional Community, https://www.ic.org

PART VI

THE REWARDS FOUND ELSEWHERE

CHAPTER TWENTY-TWO

THE BIG KAHUNA: SHELTER

The price of anything is the amount of life you exchange for it.
—Henry D. Thoreau

O ne of the problems we live with is called *reification*: our habit of turning a concept into something concrete. The best example here in America is that we virtually always think in terms of "home" rather than "shelter," instantly reducing the subject to conventional homes (maybe condos) and long discussions of rent or buy, prices, interest rates, and the unfairness of life.

We take pride in the process. We call it *realism*.

But *shelter* is an umbrella word. It opens thinking rather than forecloses it. It also contains the door to un-money, the currency of living that doesn't involve cash or taxes. The un-money economy is where cash expenses can be made to disappear because you choose (and dare) to live your life differently. Here are some examples.

ENJOY ECONOMIES OF SHARED LIVING

The traditional form of this is called marriage. You get married. You stay married.

Two people live under one roof, not two. They also share food, transportation, utilities, and other costs. The savings, as discussed in Chapter 3, are substantial.

How substantial?

Basically, the cost of living for a retired couple is only 40 percent greater than the cost of living for a single person. Here's how the MIT Living Wage project calculates the cost of living for a single person and a couple living where my wife and I live in Blanco County, Texas. Yes, it will cost more in Dallas, not to mention New York or Seattle!

If you don't know Texas, Blanco County is midway between Austin and San Antonio. It's in the heart of Texas Hill Country. My wife and I live here and love it. Houses and apartments are scarce. They tend to be expensive, at least for Texas.

Just don't go imagining that it's like the towns you saw in, say, *No Country for Old Men*.

According to the MIT Living Wage project, the total cost of living, excluding taxes, for a single person in this area is $36,882 a year. The cost of living for a couple is $51,715, only 40 percent higher. Table 22.1 compares the minimum cost for major expense areas for living alone or sharing as a couple. Note that the cost of shelter is almost identical while the cost of food is nearly double. Transportation is another major opportunity for savings.

If we were hoping to live in this area on Social Security alone, the results get even more interesting. With a need for a cash income of $36,882 a year as a single, an individual would need a rather high Social Security benefit (around $3,075 a month) to live independently. But it you combine

Table 22.1   The Economics of Sharing.

Expense	Single Person	Couple
Food	3,309	6,067
Medical	3,133	7,214
Shelter	10,484	10,544
Transportation	12,154	14,066
Civic	2,589	4,557
Internet and mobile	1,444	2,026
Other	3,720	7,242
Total after tax	36,882	51,715 (+ 40%)
Taxes	5,572	6,657
Pretax total	42,455	58,373 (+ 37%)

SOURCE: www.livingwage.mit.edu

two benefits of around $2,150, you'd only need to have benefits slightly above the average, about $2,000 a month.

Need I mention that "economies of shared living" isn't limited to traditional married couples? You can share with a good friend of the same or opposite sex. You can make a "Golden Girls" arrangement and find a group of people who enjoy sharing.

You make it sound intellectual by calling it an *intentional living community*.

But it doesn't matter.

It can happen by accident of shared interests.

It can happen by adversity.

Long ago, miles outside of Phoenix, I visited an RV park and saw a park model for the first time. Park models are small, manufactured homes of no more than 399 square feet that look like cottages. Going from door to door, asking to talk with the residents, I heard a lot of sad stories of job loss, cancer, and debt.

Necessity created a bond. The residents looked out for each other, shared cars, and enjoyed communal meals. Life was tough, but they found a way to make the best of it.

The wild, nationwide inflation of home prices that came out of COVID has turned a painful shelter situation into a crisis, with most households having neither the income nor the down payment to buy a home.

The good news is that we've seen more innovative thinking, and more flexibility, about our shelter in the last few years than we've seen in the last half century.

SHRINK YOUR SHELTER

We love our houses. That's why we spend so much on them. But the biggest lever on our cost of living, single or married, is how much we spend for shelter. In addition to the cost of operating, maintaining, and repairing our shelter, we also face major bills for real estate taxes and home insurance. It's a big deal.

But the COVID burst of housing inflation has started a major shift in how many Americans view shelter. Having become unaffordable to most people, other options are being explored. New options are being created.

Do some exploring on the web and you'll find thousands of pictures and articles on "tiny homes" – flatbed trailer-based homes less than eight feet wide and generally having under 150 square feet of living space.

You'll also find the park models mentioned previously. Considered as recreational vehicles, not real estate, their tax cost is modest. They usually contain one bedroom, a living room/kitchen area, and a full bathroom.

Beyond that, you can explore traditional manufactured homes. They can still be purchased for a fraction of the cost of a conventional stick-built home. A typical single-wide today has between 1,000 and 1,200 square feet. It will come with three bedrooms, two full bathrooms, a kitchen, and living room. That's larger than most modern apartments. It's also larger than the original homes of Levittown, the legendary postwar suburban development of affordable homes first built on Long Island, New York, and then elsewhere.

MANUFACTURED HOMES

The lower the original cost of the home, the lower all the related expenses of ownership are likely to be. In Florida, for instance, there are many resident-owned communities where residents share ownership of the land and control the expenses of operating their homeowner association. Own the house without a mortgage and total out-of-pocket costs can be well under $1,000 a month.

Some readers will recoil in horror, I'm sure.

But I've explored a number of these communities in Florida, on both coasts, and found them fascinating. My wife and I have bought and remodeled houses throughout our thirty years of marriage. We've covered the shelter options, ranging from a 3,500 square foot home in Dallas to a 1,100 square foot adobe house in Santa Fe.

Since 2019 we've lived in a pair of single-wides. They had been trashed, vandalized, and abandoned when we bought the property. But after examining the options, we decided it would be more fun to tear-out and remodel from the wall studs in. We love it and, trust me, we're kind of picky. (You can find pictures on my website.)

THE BUILDING BLOCKS OF UN-MONEY

Basically, the less shelter you own – as measured in square feet – the lower your out-of-pocket expenses. Every $1,200 a year of out-of-pocket expenses that you don't have equates to $1,538 of pretax interest income you don't need and about $30,000 of retirement savings you don't need. That's a lot of un-money.

This will seem trivial to affluent readers, but for the 94 percent of the population that lives in the paycheck world, increments like this are the building blocks of personal independence and retirement security.

THE BIG PICTURE

The potential benefits for young workers who replace ossified fixations on traditional homes with a flexible approach to shelter is stunning. While the sweet spot for builders has been homes larger than 3,000 square feet, the median size of new homes is about 2,200 square feet. Every reduction in size offers potential lifetime reductions in required income . . . and lifetime increases in personal freedom.

RELATED COLUMNS

Scott Burns, "The Secret of Crystal Bay," 2/27/15, https://scottburns.com/the-secret-of-crystal-bay/

Scott Burns, "Two Ways to Own a Manufactured Home," 3/6/15, https://scottburns.com/two-ways-to-own-a-manufactured-home-2

Scott Burns, "The Joy and Terror of Home Ownership," 10/22/22, https://scottburns.com/hang-in-for-home-ownership/

Scott Burns, "Too Much House at the End of Your Money?," 3/27/24, https://scottburns.com/too-much-house-at-the-end-of-your-money/

SOURCE AND REFERENCE

MIT Living Wage project, www.livingwage.mit.edu

CHAPTER TWENTY-THREE

A PENNY SAVED IS MUCH MORE THAN A PENNY EARNED

Too many people spend money they haven't earned, to buy things they don't want, to impress people that they don't like.
—Will Rogers

One of our biggest opportunities starts with paying attention. It's the opposite for most businesses. Some of their biggest opportunities start with our *not* paying attention.

Not paying attention is how we accumulate subscription bills that we seldom examine. For services that we no longer use.

Some of our habits of "small luxuries" are never measured against their long-term cost. A $12 a day Starbucks habit amounts to $360 a month. That's more than many people contribute to their company 401(k) plan.

Paying attention is a big part of the un-money economy. That's the economy of money that doesn't change hands because you make sure it remains in your hands.

LET'S WORK A COMMON EXAMPLE: SUBSCRIPTIONS

My son Oliver has a wireless internet company. He provides internet service to families and businesses in Texas Hill Country. Every month a handful of customers fail to pay their bill. He cuts them slack if they're having a tough time. But he often learns their subscriptions cost far more than their basic internet bill. This is particularly true, he notes, for sports buffs.

But you don't have to be a sports buff. Just subscribe to a media channel and forget about it. It's easy to have an extra $100 a month in media channels and other subscriptions that are seldom used or forgotten.

Now let's cancel those subscriptions and put the money back in your pocket.

MEASURING THE VALUE OF UN-MONEY

That $100 a month is after-tax money. You had to earn more to get it. How much more? It depends on your earnings and whether you are an employee, self-employed, or retired.

For an Employee

An employee would have paid the employee share of the employment tax, 7.65 percent. They might also be in the 10 to 22 percent tax bracket. That translates into a pretax cost range of $121.43 a month to $142.15.

If that doesn't get your attention, it annualizes to $1,457.16 to $1,705.80.

Put the un-money you didn't spend into an IRA. It will reduce your taxable income by that amount, shaving your tax bill by $145.72 to $375.28. That's a total of $1,602.88 to $2,081.08 for *unspending* $100 a month.

But wait! There's more!

Do you work for a company with a 50 percent match on their 401(k) plan? If so, that's worth another $801.44 to $1,040.54 or a total of $2,404.32 to $3,121.62.

For the Self-Employed

Whether fully self-employed or employed with a side gig, the fastest-growing worker group faces a particular burden. Their self-employment earnings pay the full employment tax, 15.3 percent. They might also be in the 10 to 22 percent tax bracket. The combination turns their after-tax $100 spending into as much as $159.49 of pretax spending.

Over 12 months, that's $1,913.87.

Again, the un-money multiplies further if the $100 not spent goes into an IRA.

But that isn't all!

If you're a gig worker and don't have health insurance through an employer, you have another de facto tax. It's the structure of the Affordable Care Act health insurance. It's a real break for those starting a business and having low earnings.

But as your income rises, the subsidy drops by $150 for every $1,000 increase in income. You'll experience that as though it was an extra marginal tax rate of 15 percent. As a result, your $100 of after-tax spending translates into as much as $209.64 of pretax spending or $2,515.72 a year.

For Retirees

Many retirees are entirely dependent on Social Security, so because their income is low, they don't pay federal income taxes. But our tax law has included the possibility of taxing Social Security benefits since 1983. I've been writing about this disaster for a long time. I labeled it the *tax torpedo* back in 2003, a phrase that has caught on.

Economists call this *tax incidence*. The tax is nominally on Social Security benefits. *But it would not exist without income from other sources.* Like the money you withdraw from an IRA or other tax-deferred account.

Our elected officials encouraged us to save for the future in tax-deferred plans with one hand. Then they added a special tax when we withdrew the money with the other hand. The gutless 535 in Congress practiced taxation without representation. Few taxpayers recognized how many would pay the tax 40 years later.

Yes, this was a bipartisan tax hosing. The proposal came from a Republican President (Reagan). It passed with strong support from both parties. Later, a Democratic President (Clinton) modified it. Again, it passed with strong support from both parties.

In early 2025, it seemed this dishonest tax was, finally, about to be eliminated or reduced. But it didn't happen. The politics of both parties are, yet again, all about posing and theater.

Spending $100 a month of after-tax retiree income means you need more pre-tax income. How much depends on your non-Social Security income. The average retiree Social Security benefit was about $2,000 a month in early 2025. The recent cost-of-living adjustment (COLA) was 2.8 percent. That's about $50 a month. So, not spending $100 a month is roughly on par with over two or three years of COLA increases.

Investment income of $1,200 a year would need a nest egg of about $24,000. This assumes you withdraw income at 5 percent. Any tax on benefits increases the amount.

The bottom line here is dirt simple. Being attentive to how we spend our income is a massive opportunity. It is an opportunity throughout our working lives. It is an opportunity throughout retirement.

RELATED COLUMNS

Scott Burns, "How the Tax Torpedo Hits," 2/11/2003, https://scottburns.com/how-the-tax-torpedo-hits/

Scott Burns, "Website Search for Tax Torpedo Columns," https://scottburns.com/?s=Tax+Torpedo

Scott Burns, "A Winning Proposal for Social Security," 3/9/2025, https://scottburns.com/a-winning-proposal-for-social-security/

Scott Burns, "The Supreme Grand Poohbah Saves Social Security," 5/4/2025, https://scottburns.com/the-supreme-grand-poohbah-saves-social-security/

SOURCES AND REFERENCES

Evaluation of the Hoyer/Primus proposal by Social Security Actuaries, https://www.ssa.gov/oact/solvency/HoyerPrimus_20250103.pdf

Alicia Munnell, Center for Retirement Research, "Here's a Proposal to Fix Social Security That We Could Enact Today," 1/29/2025, https://crr.bc.edu/heres-a-proposal-to-fix-social-security-that-we-could-enact-today/

Social Security evaluations of proposals for changes to Social Security, https://www.ssa.gov/oact/solvency/index.html

Social Security Trustees 2024 Report Summary, https://www.ssa.gov/oact/trsum/

CHAPTER TWENTY-FOUR

THE LIFETIME COMPOUNDING OF UN-MONEY

Compound interest is the eighth wonder of the world. He who understands it, earns it . . . he who doesn't . . . pays it.
— Albert Einstein (apocryphal)

WHEN A LUXURY CAR COSTS YOU A MILLION DOLLARS

How much is driving a luxury car worth to you? Is it worth the $1 million you could have in your retirement account if you chose to drive a Toyota Camry instead?

Here's how the numbers work.

Just as the Toyota Camry has a host of competitors in its price class, it also has cars of comparable size in the "near-luxury" class. When I searched on the web, I learned that the Lexus ES, Audi A4, BMW 3 series, Mercedes-Benz C-class, Cadillac CT4, Infiniti Q50, Volvo S60, and Genesis G80 were all considered comparable size sedans.

COMPARING CARS, CAREFULLY

Using the Edmunds' compare cars tool and comparing the average purchase price for the most popular models of the BMW 3 series, the Audi A4, and the Mercedes Benz C class sedans, I found that these cars cost $15,000 to $18,000 more than the Camry. That means an additional monthly car loan cost of $290 to $348 a month, assuming a 6 percent interest rate on a five-year car loan. (That's a bit below the interest rate for customers with prime credit scores. Others would pay more.)

How much will that cost difference accumulate to over a working career?

Yup, a cool million is easily possible. Just check the figures in Table 24.1. It shows, rounded down to the nearest dollar, how much a

Table 24.1   The High Cost of Near-Luxury.

$15k difference	6% growth	8% growth	10% growth
35 years	$415,521	$ 669,951	$1,110,490
40 years	$580,710	$1,019,431	$1,849,556
$18k difference	6% growth	8% growth	10% growth
35 years	$498,626	$ 803,940	$1,332,588
40 years	$696,851	$1,223,317	$2,219,467

Source: U.S. Securities and Exchange Commission / Public domain / https://www.investor.gov/financial-tools-calculators/calculators/compound-interest-calculator

$15,000 to $18,000 price difference between the most popular models of the 2025 Toyota Camry Hybrid and the most popular model of major "near-luxury" sedans of comparable size according to the compare cars tool on the www.Edmunds.com website.

I believe these are conservative figures. The only consideration is the difference in monthly payment. There are other differences. Fuel costs are almost double for near luxury. Not to mention higher insurance bills and greater depreciation.

Edmunds puts all the costs of ownership together in their "True Cost to Own®" five-year cost summary. The average five-year cost for the three near-luxury cars was $72,311, a whopping $34,374 greater than the $37,937 five-year cost of the Camry. The difference is $572.90 a month over those five years.

Compound that level of un-money for 35 years at 8 percent and you'll have $1,323,730.

As I said, just counting the monthly payment is conservative.

THE 401(K) BONUS, AGAIN

If you have the good fortune to also be employed with a company that has a 50 percent match for employee 401(k) contributions, you can probably add another 50 percent to the long-term accumulation figure.

You can increase the accumulation still more by keeping the car beyond five years. You won't have a payment to make, but your monthly car payment savings will continue so you'll still have the un-money income to invest. Fifty years ago, that would have been a daring choice because many cars were wrecks at 100,000 miles.

But today's cars are better built and last far longer.

With Medicare eligibility at age 65, you'd need to start making this choice at age 30 for a 35-year career or at age 25 for a 40-year career.

BUT WHAT ABOUT RETIREES?

Even if you finance the Camry over five years (and I hope you can pay cash!) the all-in cost difference of $573 a month of after-tax income required for owning one of the near luxury cars would be at least $674 a month or $8,089 a year. (This assumes a 15 percent tax rate.)

To have that much income at a 5 percent withdrawal rate you'd need an additional $161,780 in your retirement nest egg. That's not chicken feed. According to Vanguard's 2024 "How America Saves" report, only 23 percent of all savers had balances over $150,000.

THE BIG LESSON

Paying attention is important. It is step one of having some control over what happens in your life. Trust me, plenty of other things are still wildly out of our control. You won't be bored.

RELATED COLUMNS

Scott Burns, "How a Rogue Toyota Dealer Became a Marketing Agent for Tesla," 5/21/2024, https://scottburns.com/how-a-rogue-toyota-dealer-became-a-marketing-agent-for-tesla/

Scott Burns, "Shocking News! I've Gone Tesla," 1/12/2025, https://scottburns.com/shocking-news-ive-gone-tesla/

Scott Burns, "The Consumer Value of Transportation Efficiency," 5/18/2025, https://scottburns.com/the-consumer-value-of-transportation-efficiency/

SOURCES AND REFERENCES

Edmunds.com compare car tool, https://www.edmunds.com/car-comparisons/?
veh1=402033137&veh2=402035560&veh3=402047409&veh4=402049089

Investor.gov calculator tool, https://www.investor.gov/financial-tools-calculators/
calculators/compound-interest-calculator

Vanguard Retirement "How America Saves" report 2024, https://institutional.van
guard.com/content/dam/inst/iig-transformation/insights/pdf/2024/has/how_
america_saves_report_2024.pdf

CHAPTER TWENTY-FIVE

HEALTH IS ALL!

The first wealth is health.

—Ralph Waldo Emerson

A friend's father lives at Shell Point, a luxurious continuing care community in Fort Myers, Florida. He's been widowed for several years and is in his late 90s. But if you're expecting a story of misery and loneliness – like the many you can read daily in virtually any newspaper – you'll be disappointed.

When I last visited with him, he was sad about one thing. His doctor had told him to give up tennis.

He has the first wealth.

WHO KEEPS THE FIRST WEALTH?

Some will never have it. Many will lose it. There is no guarantee that you'll keep it if you have it.

But we can nudge the odds.

We can improve our chances at having a longer "health span," the number of years we live in good health. And our health span can be close to our life span. We can make decisions that will bring us closer to the proverbial "100-year carriage" described in Oliver Wendell Holmes's poem, "The Deacon's Masterpiece."

How do we do it?

The basics are simple. The hard part is living in a society that constantly promotes unhealthy living habits and terrible eating habits. The losses those habits cause are measured in *years* of health and *years* of life.

THE TOLL ISN'T EQUALLY DISTRIBUTED

You'll do better if you have a higher income than a lower one. Fortunately, the income measuring bar isn't very high. According to an analysis done by the actuaries at the Social Security Administration, people in the top half of the income distribution can expect to live five years longer than those in the bottom half. According to the 2024 Trustees report, that would be any income over about $69,000 in 2025.

The life expectancy "spread" is even larger at the extremes of the income scale. According to an analysis by the Social Security actuaries cited by the Center for Retirement Research at Boston College, those in the top 20 percent of income were likely to live 10 years longer than those in the bottom 20 percent of income.

Is it a sure thing? No, it's just a probability for the entire group.

Fortunately, we don't have to do much to put a heavy thumb on the scale of health and longevity. Here's an easy list:

- **Don't smoke.** Having first been warned by the Surgeon General of the United States more than 60 years ago, in 1964, you'd think the message would have sunk in. But it hasn't. Fewer smoke today, but the numbers are still in the millions. And millions more vape.

- **Drink alcohol in moderation.** Arguments about how little we should drink continue but the folks who create the life expectancy calculators all give credit for drinking modest amounts, hopefully with meals.

- **Watch what you eat.** Start with less red meat and more fresh fruit and vegetables. Less sugar. Less salt. The best shopping advice here comes from food writer Michael Pollan who says to "shop the periphery" of the grocery store and abandon the center aisles that contain all the processed foods with high concentrations of sugar, salt, fats, and additives.

- **Exercise moderately.** Walking is good. So is some strength/weight exercise. But you don't need to join a gym or fill your house with equipment. Just avoid being inert.

Frustrated at needing to bring reading glasses to the supermarket so you can read the encyclopedia of fine print on food containers? Then download Yuka, a consumer help app that rates packaged foods on a scale of 0 (the worst) to 100 (the best). Just be prepared for some surprises. When I went up and down the freezer aisle of Trader Joes expecting everything to be super good, I was wrong. Scores covered the entire range.

THE PAYOFF

You can test the benefits of changing your habits by using any of the many online life expectancy calculators. Using the very simple calculator on the John Hancock website, for instance, I found that a 65-year-old male who was overweight, smoked, drank, didn't exercise, and had high blood pressure and high cholesterol had a life expectancy of 74! (Note: the most detailed life expectancy calculator that I've seen is the Living-to-100 calculator. It may produce a different result, but all calculators reward better habits with higher life expectancy because that's what the data tells the actuaries.)

If the same 65-year-old stopped smoking, drank less, lost weight, exercised, and got his blood pressure and cholesterol down life expectancy soared to 97. That's a gain of 23 years just for paying attention and taking responsibility for your personal health.

And, by the way, investing the money not spent on smoking and drinking would likely pay your living expenses for all those years of additional life, depending on how early you start.

DON'T WAIT FOR HELP

I mention taking responsibility for a reason. We are a nation of consumers. Producers work hard to provide us with a multitude of products, including food products, that are designed to satisfy our desire for all the things found to be harmful. If we exercise our personal responsibility to take care of ourselves, the return on investment math for supermarkets will change.

Bad foods will start to go away. Good foods will have more shelf space. In fact, it's already happening.

We can change our world with our spending.

FORGET ABOUT LONG-TERM CARE INSURANCE

The creation of insurance – the whole idea of pooling risks – is one of the great inventions of Western civilization. It made global trade possible when voyages were done under sail and without good maps, let alone GPS. Insurance is such a great idea it's a shame it's in the hands of the insurance industry, which manages to overhype, oversell, and just plain lie about some of their most important products.

Like long-term care insurance.

This product is still sold by an ever-diminishing number of vendors, but it has a long history of class action suits, misleading projections, difficulties collecting benefits, disastrously increased premiums, and other horrors.

THE BEST SELL SCARE

"Nearly 70 percent of Americans 65 and over will require some kind of long-term care during their lifetime." That's one of the frequently used quotes salespeople use to close policy sales. What they don't mention is that it's a very broad statement. It fails to identify where the care will be received or how long it will be needed.

It turns out that there are three basic positions to take with respect to long-term care. The relatively affluent can self-insure because they likely have sufficient income and financial assets to fund long-term care, if it is needed. My test for this is simple: Check the average annual cost of nursing care in your state. If the annual cost is equal to your expected retirement income as a single person or as a couple, you can self-insure because you've got the income to pay for it.

Here's an example. The median cost of nursing care in a semiprivate room in Texas is $5,639 a month according to www.seniorliving.org. So you'd need a reliable income of about $68,000 to self-insure as a single person, $116,000 for a couple. But if you live in New York, you'll need $180,000 to $360,000.

Most individuals and couples simply can't afford private long-term care. Their only option is the nursing care provided by Medicaid.

Sandwiched in between those two groups are the people who are likely to think about buying a long-term care insurance policy. My suggestion is to think about it. But recognize the odds against needing the coverage. Far, far fewer than 70 percent of us are going to need long-term care for long enough to be financially disastrous.

WHAT THE EVIDENCE TELLS US

Evidence for this comes from a study done by RAND analyst Michael Hurd and others in 2017. Using data from the Health and Retirement Study, a long-term longitudinal study of nursing home use, they found that only 48.3 percent of people had *any* nursing home use. An average of 185.9 nights were spent in nursing homes, but 51.9 percent of those nights were completely covered. The amount of out-of-pocket spending was $12,006 or $5,253 if discounted at 3 percent to age 57, the beginning age for study participants.

See any scary numbers there?

Other figures revealed that only 31.6 percent of people in the samples had *any* lifetime out-of-pocket spending. The odds of use increased some for women, for single people, and for people who did not have daughters. But the study conclusion was clear:

"We estimate that 5 percent of individuals will experience lengthy stays costing them $47,000 or more (discounted), and that the lifetime chances of an episode longer than 100 days are approximately 27 percent."

In the face of that, paying the premiums for a long-term care policy for years or decades, facing rising premiums, disappearing sales reps, and insurance companies that typically deny claims at least once while providing no support when the policy owner needs help, seems like a very poor use of money. Rather than pay premiums, a better bet is to do what you're already doing: saving and investing for your future security.

RELATED COLUMNS

Scott Burns, "The Incredible Expanding Retirement," 7/20/1999, https://scottburns.com/the-incredible-expanding-retirement/

Scott Burns, "Retirement Planning, Part 2," 5/6/2001, https://scottburns.com/retirement-planning-part-2/

Scott Burns, "Playing Russian Roulette with Long Term Care," 12/2/2012, https://scottburns.com/playing-roulette-with-long-term-care/

Scott Burns, "Why It's a Good Thing to Live Beyond Age 75," 11/8/2015, https://scottburns.com/why-its-a-good-thing-to-live-beyond-age-75/

Scott Burns, "Shopping the Periphery," 5/2/2020, https://scottburns.com/shopping-the-periphery-applies-to-food-supplies/

Scott Burns, "Sandbagging the Pursuit of Happiness," 9/10/2022, https://scottburns.com/sandbagging-the-pursuit-of-happiness/

Scott Burns, "Life Is (Still) Worth Living After 75," 11/2/2022, https://scottburns.com/life-is-still-worth-living-after-75/

Scott Burns, "Choose: Money or Life?," 4/22/2023, https://scottburns.com/choosemoney-or-life/

Scott Burns, "The Next Top 1 Percent," 2/26/2023, https://scottburns.com/living-beyond-90/

Scott Burns, "Centenarians and the Cup of Life," 5/27/2024, https://scottburns.com/centenarians-and-the-cup-of-life/

SOURCES AND REFERENCES

John Hancock simple life expectancy calculator, https://www.johnhancock.com/
    life-insurance/life-expectancy-calculator.html

Michael Hurd, Pierre-Carl Michaud, and Susann Rohwedder, "Distribution of
    Lifetime Nursing Home Use and of Out-of-Pocket Spending," RAND,
    8/29/2017, https://www.rand.org/pubs/external_publications/EP67296.html

The Living to 100 life expectancy calculator, https://www.livingto100.com

Alicia Munnell, "This Trend Has Important Implications for Social Security's Full
    Retirement Age," Center for Retirement Research, 2/25/2025, https://crr.bc.edu/
    this-trend-has-important-implications-for-social-securitys-full-retirement-age/

The Yuka app, https://yuka.io/en/

CHAPTER TWENTY-SIX

SHOULD YOU STRIVE FOR EARLY RETIREMENT?

Americans used to be "citizens." Now we are consumers.
—Vicki Robin and Joe Dominguez,
Your Money or Your Life

One of the most popular themes of recent decades has been the FIRE movement: Financial Independence, Retire Early. For many, it's a made-to-order daydream. It serves as a great excuse to think about having free time and exploring foreign countries rather than working 9 to 5. Or much, much longer.

For some, it's an all-out mission with a tight schedule.

It's not unrealistic, either. If you enjoy a relatively good income, don't have extravagant tastes, and are willing to live at the standard of living necessary to reach your savings goal, all you must do is avoid commitments, save and invest a large portion of your income, and count off the months or years you'll need to reach your goal.

It can be done. It has been done.

The other thing you'll need to do is prepare to live in another country. Why? Because it will be a lot easier to retire early in another country than in the United States. So, it's no surprise there is an abundance of information available about living abroad as an expatriate. If you've never looked, a simple Google query is a good start, followed by a visit to YouTube.

SORRY, BUT I'M NOT ALL-IN ON THIS

Unfortunately, becoming an expat doesn't work for many. And it shouldn't. Here are some reasons:

- **You don't escape materialism by translating your wants into a foreign language.** If your only reason for moving abroad is that you can "live like a king" on the income you have, you're likely to be disappointed.
- **Children are a major complication.** Retire early candidates also face the issue of raising children while living abroad and mostly, or entirely, retired. Children are expensive. If you watch some of the expat video blogs, you'll notice that children are largely absent. Or they are adults and part of their planning is about visiting the adult kids in the United States or having them visit their expat parents in Spain, Costa Rica, Singapore, or wherever. That's a problem due to long flight and air travel costs.

- **A major question hasn't been asked.** If you find yourself wanting to retire, the first thing you should do is ask yourself what you hate about the work you do and whether you can change it so you can be happy and fulfilled with your work.

Is there a more workable life design alternative?

Yes. Evidence is starting to accumulate that many young people are looking to abandon the impossibly high living costs in our major cities. Instead, they move to a place where they can build a personal life, free from constant concerns about money. So, they move to smaller cities or just outside them. Sometimes they even move back to their old hometown, maybe even near their aging parents.

Note that only part of this is about money. The real goal is to reduce concern about money so there is time to pursue other goals and activities, like more time with family, more leisure time, and a life closer to nature.

In the end, as Vicki Robin and Joe Dominguez put it long ago, it's about *Your Money or Your Life* (Penguin Books, 2008).

ARRANGING THE LIFE YOU WANT IS EASIER THAN YOU THINK

Many years ago, my son Oliver and I were driving along a luxurious, tree-canopied street near downtown Dallas. Ollie looked around at the flow of Mercedes, BMWs, Lexus, and other luxury cars.

"These people must have a lot of money," he said.

"Or a lot of payments," I answered.

"Oh, you mean they're $50,000 dollar-a-year millionaires," he smiled.

"Yup. The fastest way to empty a room anywhere in America is to see who can pay cash," I said.

We both smiled.

At the time Ollie was struggling. Figuring out how to make a living is hard. He tried a lot of jobs. They produced a lot of funny stories:

- Like his brief career installing Christmas lights at Cabaret Royale, a Dallas strip club
- Or how a full-length poster board picture of him ended up in a conference room at CNET, where he worked (He was in helmet and riding leathers, receiving a speeding ticket somewhere between San Francisco to Santa Rosa.)
- Not to mention his brief role as a sheriff in a low-budget Austin movie that may never have been released, his time as a stunt man, or his struggle to make perfect french fries in a restaurant

In the flashy, high-income/high-spending cities, it's difficult to get past the wealth addiction that is all around you. It was hard for Ollie. It was hard for me. It's a good bet you're not finding it easy as well.

But life is on our side:

- Move to the country or an exurb and unrelenting wealth addiction disappears. It makes lower spending much easier.
- Reach age 55 or so and your spending will decline naturally, as shown by the "retirement spending smile."
- Eliminate debt, including a home mortgage, and the income you need while working or in retirement is reduced. Dramatically.
- Use the World Wide Web as your shopping cart and you'll spend less on transportation. Most of the retail stores you shop in won't have what you are looking for, or in your size, anyway.
- Use your mobile phone for your banking and you won't need to visit a bank and you'll likely be able to borrow, if necessary, at lower cost.
- Accept responsibility for your health and you'll live longer, eat better, and spend less on health care and expensive medications.

The more we live our lives as is, where is, the more we can appreciate the simple blessing of experiencing the here and now rather than losing it to what we wish life to be.

RELATED COLUMN

Scott Burns, "Seeing We Before I," 8/24/2025, https://scottburns.com/seeing-we-before-i/

Scott Burns, "Let's Call It – Reacherism," 4/7/2024, https://scottburns.com/lets-call-it-reacherism/

SOURCES AND REFERENCES

Brookes, A.C. (2022). *From Strength to Strength*. Portfolio/Penguin.
Robin, V. and Dominguez, J. (2008). *Your Money or Your Life*. Penguin Books.
Slater, P. (1980). *Wealth Addiction*. E.P. Dutton.

PART VII

MORE COUCH POTATO COOKBOOK – EXACTLY HOW TO DO IT

CHAPTER TWENTY-SEVEN

THE BASIC COUCH POTATO COOKBOOK

Cooking is at once child's play and adult joy. And cooking done with care is an act of love.

—Craig Claiborne

Managing your money is a lot like home cooking. Most of us have favorites that we make repeatedly. We do this because it's quick, simple, and we always enjoy it. While we may enjoy cooking some foods for special occasions, they are far too much bother to make frequently. We'd rather spend our time on something else.

That's the key to Couch Potato investing. And it's a good thing.

Recently, the stockanalysis.com website showed that some 378 firms offered exchange-traded funds (ETFs). Worse, the number of American ETFs is now 3,822 according to YCharts.com, an investment data website. That's *more* than the 2,132 domestic and international stocks listed on the

New York Stock Exchange. It's also more than the 3,289 stocks listed on NASDAQ.

Most ETFs deserve no attention whatsoever. They are instruments for speculators, designed by Wall Street to gather profits and encourage short-term trading. I could list some of the more ludicrous ETFs for you, but it isn't worth your time or mine.

THE COUCH POTATO PORTFOLIO YOU START FROM . . . OR GO BACK TO

As shown in Chapter 12, there are abundant reasons to favor the simplest Couch Potato portfolio. It will provide you with a long-term return that will beat 80 percent, or more, of managed funds. Even more on a risk-adjusted basis. It's also the lowest cost, most tax-efficient, and easiest to manage because all you need to do is divide by 2 once a year to rebalance the portfolio.

You can't even beg off if using numbers is a challenge. You can use an online or handheld calculator to do the division, if need be.

The portfolio is as follows:

½ US Total Stock Market Index fund ETF

½ US Total Bond Market Index fund ETF

You can build it in *any* brokerage account, with no commissions. Sometimes you'll get a cash bonus for opening the account. I suggest, however, that you open an account with an established discount brokerage firm. It's the only way to avoid most (but not all) of the effort traditional firms make to get you committed to something that is better for them, but worse for you.

As a practical matter, five firms account for most of the assets in ETFs. Only four of them provide the kind of low-cost, low-turnover, major index ETFs that are suitable for Couch Potato investors:

- **BlackRock iShares.** The firm offers 469 funds at an average expense of 0.30 percent and has $3.354 trillion in ETF assets.
- **Vanguard.** The original index fund company has 91 ETFs with an average expense of 0.08 percent and has $3.213 trillion in ETF assets.
- **State Street.** The firm that launched the first ETF in 1993 has 160 funds at an average expense of 0.27 percent and has $1.538 trillion in ETF assets.
- **Schwab.** The first discount broker and first mutual fund marketplace firm has 33 funds with an average expense of 0.12 percent and has $426 billion in ETF assets.

A handful of other firms deserve attention, but largely as footnotes. I'll discuss them later.

While iShares ETFs have an average expense of 0.30 percent and State Street averages 0.27 percent, both firms are like Schwab in offering core ETFs that are head-to-head priced with Vanguard's pace-setting low expenses. State Street, for instance, has core ETFs priced at 0.03 of assets. BlackRock's iShares core ETFs also cost 0.03 percent. Schwab, too.

If you stick with the basic Couch Potato portfolio, you'll be managing your money at a total cost of 0.03 percent a year.

It's hard to get less expensive than that.

IS THERE A DIFFERENCE IN RISK OR RETURN?

As a practical matter, these funds are virtually interchangeable. Table 27.1 shows the basic return, risk, and expense figures for the eight ETFs that are

Table 27.1   The Best Providers of Basic Couch Potato Portfolio ETFs.

TOTAL US STOCK MARKET ETFs				
	Vanguard	**BlackRock iShares**	**State Street**	**Schwab**
Metric/fund	VTI	ITOT	SPTM	SCHB
Annualized return	12.50%	12.53%	12.65%	12.99%
Std. deviation	15.17	15.76	15.58	15.87
M2	12.78	12.81	13.01	12.78
Exp. ratio	0.03%	0.03%	0.03%	0.03%
TOTAL US BOND MARKET ETFs				
Metric/fund	BND	AGG	SPAB	SCHZ
Annualized return	1.30%	1.32%	1.26%	1.24%
Std. deviation	5.18	5.12	5.09	5.19
M2	0.79	0.81	0.62	0.61
Exp. ratio	0.03%	0.03%	0.03%	0.03%

SOURCES: Adapted from www.stockanalysis.com and www.portfoliovisualizer.com

the best choices for a Couch Potato portfolio. The Modigliani-Modigliani (M2), as explained in Chapter 13, is a tool that adjusts returns to provide the return if adjusted for differences in risk by adding risk-free cash until risk is equal. These figures are for the 10-year period ending 31 December 2024. The only fund that doesn't have a record that long is the Schwab aggregate bond market ETF, ticker SCHZ. But if you use the compare funds tool on www.stockanalysis.com you'll see that it provides a remarkably similar risk and return since its later inception. The return and risk figures change with each period, so it is important to have the same period for each comparison chart. The 10-year period is the only period available for free to users of www.portfoliovisualizer.com.

THE LAST FULL MEASURE

Is there anything else to consider?

Yes: size – assets under management in each fund. The greater the assets, the greater the number of shareholders and the greater the volume of trading. That means more liquidity and an opportunity for better execution when you place a buy or sell order. In this arena, BlackRock's iShares and Vanguards ETF funds are the vehicles of choice. Their assets under management dwarf the assets in funds with the same stocks in other firms.

While Vanguard and iShares have $467 billion and $67 billion, respectively, in each of their US total stock market ETFs, State Street has only $10 billion, and Schwab has only $32 billion. It's the same with their bond market ETFs. While iShares and Vanguard have over $120 billion in each of their US total bond market ETFs, State Street and Schwab have only $8 billion each.

Of all these firms, only Schwab also has actual branch offices you can visit – over 400 of them. That's nearly twice as many as Fidelity.

FEDERAL EMPLOYEES AND THE THRIFT SAVINGS PLAN

The federal government is our nation's largest employer. According to the Bureau of Labor Statistics about 3 million civilian workers were employed plus another 1.3 million active-duty military and 600,000 US Postal Service workers – nearly 5 million people. Since most federal employees are eligible for Social Security and a government-defined benefit pension, as well as the very low-cost Thrift Savings Plan (TSP), they are the largest group of people who are likely to have all three legs of the traditional retirement stool: Social Security, a pension and retirement savings.

A Couch Potato portfolio can be easily made by electing to put equal amounts into the G Fund and the C Fund. It will not be entirely identical to the Couch Potato portfolio because the two funds are somewhat different from a total stock market index ETF and a total bond market ETF. But the performance should be quite similar.

The C Fund duplicates an index of the S&P 500 rather than the total market. The S&P 500 represents about 80 percent of total US market capitalization. The G Fund is built on an index of Treasury obligations but is also guaranteed to be of stable value. It will return a bit more than a money market fund while having none of the risk of a total bond market index fund.

THE BIGGEST DANGER FOR TSP PARTICIPANTS

Government employees have two sources of promise-based income: Social Security and their government-defined benefit pension. Long-term service employees are likely to be able to cover their core expenses with those two income sources. This means they can use their TSP accounts to accumulate financial assets that will provide them with flexibility and liquidity in retirement.

Unfortunately, that's exactly the opposite of what many commission-based vendors try to sell government employees as they approach retirement. Instead of continuing in the low-cost TSP options or rolling over to a low-cost IRA plan, the salespeople offer complicated, high-commission insurance products that lock up their money and reduce their flexibility.

(The same thing also happens to many public school teachers in 403[b] plans. They are offered expensive investment products, often by former teachers.)

THE FOOTNOTE FIRMS

It's good to be aware of three other firms that offer ETFs, all for different reasons.

Fidelity

As the largest provider of 401(k) services, there is a good chance that more readers have accounts at Fidelity than have accounts anywhere else. In addition, the firm has 217 offices across the United States, which means you don't have to be a 100 percent digital person to do business with them. The firm also has a dozen international investor centers. While their in-house ETF offerings are limited, you can still buy and sell, commission-free, all the ETFs previously mentioned.

Decades ago, when Ned Johnson was still alive, I asked him why he didn't take Fidelity public. "I couldn't spend the amount I am investing in software development if we had to answer to Wall Street analysts," he said. So, he kept Fido private, and it remains so. His willingness to spend heavily on software development provides investors with one of the easiest to use and most informative computer screens in existence. This makes your life as an investor easier. Another Johnson innovation was the creation of the first brokerage charitable gift fund, a tool that enables investors of all sizes to put aside funds for charitable giving.

Dimensional

The most scholarly of all the fund providers, Dimensional is now offering ETF versions of their mutual funds that have typically only been available through registered investment advisor firms. The distinction means a retail investor can buy these funds without the added expense of an investment advisor. For most readers this is a sideshow, but Dimensional has grown from a tiny institutional firm to an enormous company serving individual investors, easily surpassing most of the legacy brokerage firms that continued to focus on yield to broker.

Capital Group

The American Funds have offered some of the most successful and best-managed mutual funds in the country, always at reasonable cost for broker-distributed funds. I've known brokers who have built their entire careers using these funds. Now they are offering ETF versions that are more tax efficient. As with Dimensional, the ETFs offer a side door to employ their funds without the commission cost of a brokerage account or a management fee.

RELATED COLUMNS

Scott Burns, "Setting a Higher Standard for Lifecycle Funds," 3/21/2006, https://scottburns.com/setting-a-higher-standard-for-lifecycle-funds/

Scott Burns, "First, Do No Harm," 11/5/2006, https://scottburns.com/first-do-no-harm/

SOURCES AND REFERENCES

Stockanalysis.com rank ordered list of largest EFT firms, https://stockanalysis.com/etf/provider/

ISHARES

Stockanalysis.com list of iShares ETFs, https://stockanalysis.com/etf/provider/blackrock/

ITOT, https://stockanalysis.com/etf/itot/

AGG, https://stockanalysis.com/etf/agg/

World x US: IEFA, https://stockanalysis.com/etf/iefa/

Large growth: IWF, https://stockanalysis.com/etf/iwf/

Large value: IWD, https://stockanalysis.com/etf/iwd/

Screen for iShares ETF, https://www.ishares.com/us/products/etf-investments#/?productView=etf&pageNumber=1&sortColumn=totalNetAssets&sortDirection=desc&dataView=keyFacts

iShares ETF ladder building tool, https://www.blackrock.com/us/financial-professionals/tools/ibonds

SCHWAB

Stockanalysis.com list of Schwab ETFs, https://stockanalysis.com/etf/provider/charles-schwab/

Total US SCHB, https://stockanalysis.com/etf/schb/

Total Bond SCHZ, https://stockanalysis.com/etf/schz/

World x US SCHF, https://stockanalysis.com/etf/schf/

Large Growth SCHG, https://stockanalysis.com/etf/schg/

Large Value SCHV, https://stockanalysis.com/etf/schv/

STATE STREET

Stockanalysis.com list of State Street ETFs, https://stockanalysis.com/etf/provider/state-street/

Screener, https://stockanalysis.com/etf/screener/

SPTM, https://stockanalysis.com/etf/sptm/

SPAB, https://stockanalysis.com/etf/spab/

SPDW, https://stockanalysis.com/etf/spdw/

SPYV, https://stockanalysis.com/etf/spyv/

SPYG, https://stockanalysis.com/etf/spyg/

THRIFT SAVINGS PLAN

"Investor Alert: Fraudsters May Target Federal Government Employee Retirement Plan Participants," Investor.gov, 7/31/2017, https://www.investor.gov/introduction-investing/general-resources/news-alerts/alerts-bulletins/investor-alerts/investor-26

Thrift Savings Plan website, https://www.tsp.gov

VANGUARD

Stockanalysis.com list of Vanguard ETFs, https://stockanalysis.com/etf/provider/vanguard/

VTI, https://stockanalysis.com/etf/vti/

BND, https://stockanalysis.com/etf/bnd/

VXUS, https://stockanalysis.com/etf/vxus/

VIG, https://stockanalysis.com/etf/vig/

VTV, https://stockanalysis.com/etf/vtv/

CHAPTER TWENTY-EIGHT

STILL MORE COUCH POTATO COOKBOOK

When trillions of dollars are managed by Wall Streeters charging high fees, it will usually be the managers who reap outsized profits, not the clients.

—Warren Buffett

G oing beyond a dirt-simple two-fund portfolio is a constant temptation. It can also be a slippery slope into chaos. At its worst, adding more pieces to your portfolio will create what some advisors call *scattered asset syndrome*. That's what happens when you invest in things because your golf buddy stockbroker has an interesting idea or your brother-in-law had a good tip, or the pious insurance agent at your church convinced you that you needed more certainty.

Whatever the cause, the result is monthly statements from multiple sources, difficulty in knowing exactly how much of your money is committed to any investment and the kind of mess you don't want to leave to your adult children.

So, as in Chapter 13, I write about more complex portfolios with reluctance. The data, however, shows that when risk/volatility is considered, the simplest portfolio is the best option. You'll need to have a compelling sense of secular change to go beyond the basic Couch Potato portfolio.

BUT . . .

As I write this, two major forces indicate that adding a third or fourth piece to your portfolio might finally work better than utter simplicity.

The first of those forces is high domestic stock market valuation and the record concentration of asset values in technology stocks. The most frequently referenced metric for stock market prices is the Shiller CAPE ratio. CAPE stands for cyclically adjusted price-to-earnings ratio based on the average inflation-adjusted price-to-earnings (PE) ratio over the preceding 10 years. The long-term median for this ratio is 16. The current figure is nearly 36, close to the all-time high of 44 reached in 1999.

You know what happened after that.

If stocks revert to their long-term median (as opposed to falling to their historic low of about 5), equities will decline more than 50 percent.

This assumes earnings don't decline as well. We've had a long expansion.

IT'S AN INDICATOR, NOT A PREDICTOR

This doesn't mean stocks will drop by half tomorrow morning. The Schiller CAPE ratio isn't predictive in the short term. But it has shown a high probability of below-average returns for longer time periods going forward.

It's possible that a tilt to value stocks – stocks selling at relatively low multiples of earnings, usually (but not always) offering higher than average dividends will provide higher (relative) returns than the total stock market. (Note: This doesn't always mean they will return more. It could mean they lose less.)

GLOBAL POWER SHIFT

The second force is what appears to be a gigantic realignment of geopolitical forces that was put in motion with the broad and unilateral declaration of large tariffs on our trading partners, friends and foes alike. The United States has been the central power in world trade since the end of World War II. We benefit enormously from being the reserve currency of the world.

We've also provided a defense security blanket that other nations failed to provide for themselves. The biggest loser in this realignment is likely to be our country: We'll be able to trade fewer inflated paper dollars for actual goods.

We'll lose trade we would otherwise have had. Other nations will need to hold fewer dollars. This will (and has) raised our interest rates because we'll have to invest in our own rising debt. Alternatively, inflation could rise from a combination of tariffs and federal reserve actions to buy government debt in lieu of foreign buyers.

Whatever happens, it's all *assumptions* about a future that is unknown.

THE CHOICE

Since foreign stocks are selling at lower PE ratios than domestic stocks while offering higher dividend yields, we can accommodate both forces by betting that the three-part portfolio Taylor Larimore advocated (see Chapter 14) is the portfolio of the future.

As I write this the total US Stock Market ETFs are yielding about 1.3 percent, less than half of the 2.9 percent yield of the major World ex US indices – the ETFs like VXUS and IEFA that invest globally, excluding the United States. They have trailed the US market horribly over the last 5, 10, and more years. But their most recent returns have, at long last, beaten US returns. Institutional investors have said this was coming for decades. Table 28.1 compares the major metrics for the two largest World ex US Index ETFs and Vanguard Total Stock Market Index. While price volatility was comparable, US returns were more than double the international alternative – but the PE multiples difference is huge.

Table 28.2 shows the same metrics comparing two major domestic value stock ETFs with the Vanguard Total Stock Market Index ETF. While price volatility was similar, total US market annualized returns were about 50 percent larger – but the PE ratio difference gives pause. As you can see, the two value-oriented ETFs trailed the Total Stock Market Index by a substantial margin.

Table 28.1 Domestic Equities Versus International Equities.

Metric/Fund	VXUS	IEFA	VTI
Annualized return	5.09%	5.46%	12.50%
Std. deviation	15.18	15.31	15.77
M2	6.18	6.51	12.78
Exp. ratio	0.05	0.07	0.03
Yield (6/25)	2.92	2.97	1.29
PE ratio (6/25)	15.83	16.03	24.52

SOURCES: Adapted from www.portfoliovisualizer.com and www.stockanalysis.com

Table 28.2   Total Domestic Equities Versus Domestic Value Equities.

Metric/Fund	VTV	IWD	VTI
Annualized return	9.99%	8.31%	12.50%
Std. deviation	14.97	15.74	15.77
M2	10.89	9.06	12.78
Exp. ratio	0.04	0.19	0.03
Yield (6/25)	2.30	1.86	1.29
PE ratio (6/25)	18.83	19.08	24.52

Sources: www.portfoliovisualizer.com 10 year figures to end 2024; yield and PE figures are June 2025 figures from www.stockanalysis.com

VARIATIONS ON A COUCH POTATO

Now let's see if adding international equities or domestic value stocks would have improved the basic Couch Potato portfolio. Table 28.3 compares metrics for three portfolios: the simple 50/50 Couch Potato portfolio and adding either international equities or domestic value stocks. Since all parts are added in equal portions to keep things simple, the three-part

Table 28.3   Couch Potato Portfolio Versus Added International or Added Domestic Value.

Asset Class Allocation	50/50	33/34/33	33/34/33
Metric/Portfolio	VTI/BND	VTI/BND/VXUS	VTI/BND/VTV
Annualized return	7.05%	6.40%	8.04%
Std. deviation	9.19	10.68	10.65
M2	10.95	8.99	**11.23**
Exp. ratio	0.03	0.037	0.033

portfolios are 66 percent equity, which is substantially greater than the 50 percent of the basic Couch Potato. The added price volatility, however, brings a gain many investors may want to consider – at least with domestic value stocks. Unless there is a major geopolitical shift, international equities add price volatility while decreasing return.

In Table 28.4, the equities/bonds allocation remains 50/50. Adding domestic value reduces portfolio return and lowers price volatility – but not by enough to make it compelling.

Without a crystal ball, the basic 50/50 Couch Potato portfolio remains the choice that provides simplicity and a reasonable return.

That's all we need to do.

Remember: *Everything* else in life is more important!

When I find that hard to remember, I listen to King Harvest sing "Dancing in the Moonlight."

Try it.

Table 28.4   Couch Potato Portfolio Versus Proportionately Weighted Alternatives.

Asset Class Allocation	50/50	25/50/25	25/50/25
Metric/Portfolio	VTI/BND	VTI/BND/VXUS	VTI/BND/VTV
Annualized return	7.50%	5.61%	6.84%
Std. deviation	9.19	8.85	8.73
M2	**10.95**	8.21	10.35
Exp. ratio	0.03%	0.035	0.033

Source: www.portfoliovisualizer.com, 10-year figures ending 12/24.

RELATED COLUMN

Scott Burns, "The Simplicity Manifesto," 3/31/2019, https://scottburns.com/the-simplicity-manifesto/

SOURCES AND REFERENCES

King Harvest, "Dancing in the Moonlight" on YouTube, https://www.youtube.com/watch?v=g5JqPxmYhlo
Schiller CAPE ratio graph, https://www.gurufocus.com/economic_indicators/56/sp-500-shiller-cape-ratio
Schiller CAPE 10 PE ratio, https://www.multpl.com/shiller-pe

PART VIII

THE RESEARCH AND DATA THAT SUPPORTS EVERYTHING I'VE SAID

CHAPTER TWENTY-NINE

WHY COUCH POTATO INVESTING MAKES SENSE: A TOUR OF THE RESEARCH AND DATA

L ife is full of awakenings. You've probably had a few, so you know. Some are rude. Some are wonderful. One of the least discussed awakenings is the moment we realize other humans have been thinking and learning about how the world works since early humans first marked cave walls with drawings.

The amount we've learned about ourselves, and the world, is staggering. And it is growing at an exponential rate. There is no way to keep up. That reality is demonstrated in the bibliographies at the end of some books.

My favorite recent example is *The Technological Republic: Hard Power, Soft Belief, and the Future of the West* by Alexander C. Karp and Nicholas W. Zamiska (Crown Currency, 2025), the founders of Palantir. It's an amazing reframing of our history, particularly recent decades.

The text clocks in at 220 pages. The bibliography starts at page 221 and goes on to page 284! That's 64 pages of citations. This is the kind of bedrock scholarship required if your goal is to change America and the fate of Western civilization.

Fortunately, my goal is more modest. It is to open a door to an easier, better life through low-cost index investing. So, what follows is a casual bus tour, not a mountain climb, of *some* of the research and data that supports the simplicity I have urged on readers for decades.

I can assure you that is not complete. But it is more than enough.

INTRODUCTION: AN EASY STROLL TO INVESTMENT SUCCESS AND A BETTER LIFE

Mood is important. So if the lyrics of Don Henley's "Take It Easy" don't establish a great spring day mood, please visit YouTube and listen, https://www.youtube.com/watch?v=AaBw37-nWaY&list=RDAaBw37-nWaY&start_radio=1. Know that we're working our way toward King Harvest and "Dancing in the Moonlight," https://www.youtube.com/watch?v=g5JqPxmYhlo.

Chapter 1: What Happens When an Aspiring Astronaut and Biologist Becomes a Writer

Arthur C. Clarke's short story "Superiority" was published in 1951 and is at least as relevant today as it was then, https://www.baen.com/Chapters/1439133476/1439133476___5.htm.

If you've never visited the Morningstar website, now would be a good time, https://www.morningstar.com.

And you can read Bill Bengen's most recent book, *A Richer Retirement: Supercharging the 4% Rule to Spend More and Enjoy More* (Wiley, 2025).

PART I: THE HUMAN LIFE CYCLE: WE SHARE MORE THAN YOU THINK

Chapter 2: What Seven Billion Humans Want

We all want to love and to be loved, a fact that shows up in Current Population Reports: "Number, Timing, and Duration of Marriages and Divorces: 2016," https://www.census.gov/content/dam/Census/library/publications/2021/demo/p70-167.pdf.

But our pursuit of money and the growing insecurity of income sources has changed our mating habits. That reality shows up in a lower birth rate, as seen in National Center for Health Statistics, "U.S. Fertility Rate Drops to Another Historic Low," 4/25/2024. https://www.cdc.gov/nchs/pressroom/nchs_press_releases/2024/20240525.htm. This results in frustration for many families who actually want more children, as demonstrated in this study by the Institute for Family Studies, "How Many Kids Do Women Want?," 6/1/2018, https://ifstudies.org/blog/how-many-kids-do-women-want#:~:text=That%20personal%20ideal%20may%20still,%2C%20in%20others%2C%20it's%20lower.

The result is insecurity all around.

Chapter 3: Measuring the Big Sameness in Cash: The Revised Equivalence Scale

When you examine the cost of living over time for most people who seek a person to love and nurture children, you learn that we've never had a lot of our income to spend on ourselves because it went to raising children. This is demonstrated by the Revised Equivalence Scale, one of many tools for measuring household expenses, "Revised Equivalence Scale: For Estimating Equivalent Incomes or Budget Costs by Family Type," 11/1968, https://fraser.stlouisfed.org/files/docs/publications/bls/bls_1570-2_1968.pdf. It's shown even more starkly in the USDA figures for the cost of raising a child, "USDA The Cost of Raising a Child" graphic, https://fns-prod.azureedge.us/sites/default/files/resource-files/crc_infographic-2015.2.pdf.

Chapter 4: The Big Sameness in Cash: The Reverse Engineering Way

We may climb a mountain of money in our working life, but an exercise in reverse engineering shows that it makes the retirement descent a lot easier as shown in the Aon Consulting, "2008 Replacement Ratio Study," https://www.aon.com/about-aon/intellectual-capital/attachments/human-capital-consulting/RRStudy070308.pdf.

Other factors, like the amount of income we must commit to our various debts, reduce the retirement cost of living still further. And that's before discovering the "retirement spending smile," https://www.soa.org/globalassets/assets/files/resources/essays-monographs/2014-living-to-100/mono-li14-1a-blanchett.pdf.

Other researchers, like Andrew G. Biggs, have estimated that Social Security covers most retirement spending for a large percentage of retirees, Andrew G. Biggs and Glenn R. Springstead, "Alternate Rates for Social Security Benefits and Retirement Income," 10/2008, https://www.aon.com/about-aon/intellectual-capital/attachments/human-capital-consulting/RRStudy070308.pdf.

Chapter 5: The Snatch Defeat from the Jaws of Victory Industry

Why is it that the financial services industry looks at the massive increase in life expectancy in the last century and only sees a financial problem? The statistics of gained life expectancy are amazing and can be seen in the National Vital Statistics Reports, "United States Life Tables, 2018," 11/17/2020, https://www.cdc.gov/nchs/data/nvsr/nvsr69/nvsr69-12-508.pdf.

If there is a problem, it is that the gain in life expectancy is not well distributed. And in recent years, life expectancy for the poor has declined as witnessed in this presentation by Anne Case and Angus Deaton, https://cehd.uchicago.edu/?p=2796.

Chapter 6: The Sublime Blessing of Death

If higher life expectancies for those with higher incomes are a financial problem, consider how difficult undeadness must be for vampires. There are lots of places to explore the income/life expectancy issue but this Congressional Research Service paper is a good, if nerdy, start, https://www.congress.gov/crs-product/R44846.

PART II: THE LONG, GLORIOUS HISTORY OF INVESTMENT FAILURE

Chapter 7: Weston Wellington and the Wisdom of Not Guessing the Future

Weston Wellington shows, in a decades-long series of magazine and newspaper headlines, that staying invested is the best course. But if you have doubts, the whole idea has been taken even further with absolute "do nothing" investing as shown in this column by Morningstar's John Rekenthaler, "More Lessons from the Do Nothing Portfolio," 4/20/2023, https://www.morningstar.com/columns/rekenthaler-report/more-lessons-do-nothing-portfolio.

Chapter 8: The Legion of Amazing, but Temporary, Heroes

The easy read here is Michael Batnick's *Big Mistakes: The Best Investors and Their Worst Investments* (Wiley/Bloomberg, 2018). But if you're tenacious and love statistics and probability, you can go lots further and read Michael Mauboussin's "The Success Equation: Untangling Skill and Luck in Business, Sports and Investing," *Harvard Business Review Press*, 2012. You could also read poker player Annie Duke's *Thinking in Bets: Making Smarter Decisions When You Don't Have All the Facts* (Penguin Portfolio, 2019).

But if you want to avoid the math complexity, just read my column citing a story in number theorist Jordan Ellenberg's book, *How Not to Be Wrong: The Power of Mathematical Thinking* (Penguin Press, 2014), about solving the problem of protecting aircraft in World War II, https://scottburns.com/the-missing-bullet-holes-problem/.

Chapter 9: Bogleheads and Fighting Back

To find moral support, just visit the John C. Bogle Center for Financial Literacy at https://boglecenter.net or the Bogleheads Facebook page at https://www.facebook.com/Bogleheads/. As an alternative, read any book written by John C. Bogle, the founder of Vanguard.

Chapter 10: Turn Off, Tune Out, and Drop In (With Apologies to Timothy Leary)

To find out how much of your time is being stolen by all the apps on your phone, visit https://backlinko.com/screen-time-statistics. If what you learn there moves you to rebel against being the unwilling victim being water boarded by a plethora of marketing funnels, read Jaron Lanier's *Ten Arguments for Deleting Your Social Media Accounts Right Now* (Henry Holt, 2018).

PART III: HOW TO INVEST YOUR SAVINGS

Chapter 11: ETFs: You Can Now Invest Almost for Free

Money goes where it is treated well. That's why exchange-traded funds (ETFs) have been displacing traditional mutual fund investments, with the very largest amounts of new money going into a handful of very large, very liquid, very low-cost ETFs that are ideal for Couch Potato investors. You can see the growth of ETFs on the FRED website, https://fred.stlouisfed.org/series/BOGZ1FL564090005Q. You can also read about the ongoing failure of managed funds to beat their index in this column about the SPIVA research from 2022, https://scottburns.com/index-funds-beat-managed-funds-again-and-again/.

Chapter 12: The Simplicity Portfolio – Couch Potato Investing

The SPIVA research has shown, twice a year for 20 years, that managed funds can't beat their appointed index, and you can see the most recent report at https://www.spglobal.com/spdji/en/research-insights/spiva/. You can understand why this happens in very few pages by reading Charlie Ellis's "The Losers Game," free, on this website, https://www.tandfonline.com/doi/epdf/10.2469/faj.v31.n4.19?needAccess=true.

Chapter 13: Occam's Razor: Riffs on the Couch Potato Portfolio That Don't Work

If you only measure the return on your investment, you haven't got the whole story. You also need to consider risk. There are lots of ways of doing that, but my favorite is called Modigliani-Modigliani, or M2. You can read about how it is defined on Wikipedia, https://en.wikipedia.org/wiki/Modigliani_risk-adjusted_performance#:~:text=Modigliani%20risk%2Dadjusted%20performance%20(also,(e.g.%2C%20the%20market). As this chapter shows, the simplest Couch Potato portfolio provided an absolute return very close to some alternatives but was the best when adjusted for risk.

Chapter 14: Riffs on the Couch Potato Portfolio to Consider

This chapter uses M2 to examine two popular alternatives to the basic Couch Potato portfolio. But it finds that the basic Couch Potato portfolio wins on a risk-adjusted basis over the riskier Margarita portfolio. So, is there ever a reason to consider adding a slug of international equities? Only if you are convinced that the status of the United States as a global power is in a long decline.

Another option that some advocate is to replace your bond segment with a ladder of US Treasury securities. The case for doing that, as this is written, is good. You can learn about building ladders using BlackRock term ETFs at https://www.blackrock.com/us/financial-professionals/tools/ibonds.

For some reinforcement on the value of utter simplicity, read my Simplicity Manifesto at https://scottburns.com/the-simplicity-manifesto/.

Chapter 15: The Bonus of Low-Cost Compounding While Growing

Low-cost index investing helps your savings grow faster. You can measure by how much with a simple tool like the Schwab Moneywise Compound Savings Calculator at https://www.schwabmoneywise.com/compound-savings-calculator.

The difference will amount to actual *years* of your final income. Taking advantage of nearly free investing is important to your future. If you want to see just how important, you'll need to go beyond spreadsheets and use a tool like Larry Kotlikoff's MAXIFI Planner, which you'll find at https://maxifiplanner.com.

This tool can't predict the future, but it can give you an accurate picture of your lifetime consumption under different assumptions. You can learn more by reading *Spend 'Til the End: The Revolutionary Guide to Raising Your Living Standard – Today and When You Retire*, one of the three books I coauthored with Kotlikoff (Simon & Schuster, 2008).

Chapter 16: The Bonus of Low-Cost Investing While Spending

When investment fees aren't considered as part of your annual withdrawals, the survival of your portfolio is reduced. The probability of running out of money is increased. You can explore life expectancy by downloading financial planner Michael Kitces calculator, https://www.kitces.com/?s =Life+expectancy+calculator&submit=&by-author=&by-category=& from-date=&to-date=.

Portfolio survival rates at different expense levels can be explored using the www.portfoliovisualizer.com website. Unfortunately, the ability to vary expense levels requires their most expensive subscription.

Chapter 17: Can You Spend More?

My wealth scoreboard regularly shows that people start to feel free to distribute assets rather than accumulate them at different ages. People in the top 1 percent to top 25 percent in wealth distribute in their 60s while people at the median distribute in their late 70s, as shown in this column, https://scottburns.com/the-post-covid-wealth-scoreboard/.

But the best simple tool for estimating the maximum you can distribute each year is found in an article by M. Barton Waring and Larry Siegel, "The Only Spending Rule Article You'll Ever Need" (July 2014). It is based on calculating your life expectancy each year and distributing according to that. Much higher, particularly at higher ages, than required minimum distributions.

PART IV: THE PROOF IS IN THE PUDDING

Chapter 18: The Pudding Reports: It's All About the Cash

My "Pudding Reports" are updated annually and show how much actual cash is left after making inflation-adjusted withdrawals over time periods from 1 year to 30 years. They are reassuring and verify that Bill Bengen's spending rule of a bit over 4 percent is a good rule of thumb for retirement spending. You can generate your own reports, with your own portfolio by subscribing to www.portfoliovisualizer.com.

PART V: THE REWARDS OF SIMPLICITY FOR ACTUAL PEOPLE

Chapter 19: How Average Becomes Superior

The SPIVA reports routinely demonstrate that the longer you invest, the greater the probability that owning index funds instead of managed funds will be the better choice. You can read the 2024 SPIVA report at https://www.spglobal.com/spdji/en/documents/spiva/spiva-us-year-end-2024.pdf.

To read all the columns I've written over the years on the SPIVA reports, go to https://scottburns.com/?s=SPIVA.

Chapter 20: The Unspoken Forms of Capital

The financial services industry focuses on our financial wealth but ignores other kinds of wealth that are very important: time, social, mental, and physical. You can read about these in Sahil Bloom's *The 5 Types of Wealth: A Transformative Guide to Design Your Dream Life* (Ballantine Books, 2025).

Sadly, my own book on the nonmoney economy, *Home, Inc.: The Hidden Wealth and Power of the American Household* (Doubleday, 1975), is out of print. But you can read an updated version of Vicki Robin and Joe Dominguez's *Your Money or Your Life: 9 Steps to Transforming Your Relationship with Money and Achieving Financial Independence* (Penguin Books, 2008).

For a more scholarly examination of the issues we face, read Juliet B. Schor's *The Overspent American: Why We Want What We Don't Need* (Harper Perennial, 1999) or *The Overworked American: The Unexpected Decline of Leisure* (Basic Books, 1992). Both books were published in the 1990s but are even more relevant today than they were then.

Chapter 21: Rising Above Serfdom in an Age of Neo-Feudalism

One of the more persistent dystopian views of our collective future is called *neo-feudalism* in which giant corporations are the equivalents of ancient kingdoms but far more powerful, best described in Joel Kotkin's *"The Coming of Neo-Feudalism: A Warning to the Global Middle Class* (Encounter Books, 2020). The best way to avoid serfdom is to build sources of "un-money": receiving benefits in noncash forms that escape taxation and the coercive reach of government and corporations.

A column on that subject is "How to Join the Un-Money Economy and Prosper,": https://scottburns.com/how-to-join-the-un-money-economy-and-prosper/.

PART VI: THE REWARDS FOUND ELSEWHERE

Chapter 22: The Big Kahuna: Shelter

Our biggest single expense, all our lives, is the cost of housing – keeping a roof over our heads. If we open our minds to "shelter" and stop thinking about home ownership, we can start to liberate ourselves from the commitments that imprison us in a lifetime of debt. Then we can start exploring alternatives that will reduce our shelter spending during our working lives and continue into retirement. These alternatives include RV parks, owner-occupied manufactured home parks, tiny homes, and intentional communities.

One tool for examining low-cost living is the MIT Living Wage project, www.livingwage.mit.edu.

You can start to understand the differences by reading this column, https://scottburns.com/two-ways-to-own-a-manufactured-home-2.

Chapter 23: A Penny Saved Is Much More Than a Penny Earned

Whether you are an employee, self-employed, or retired, taxes on your income make a very big difference in your standard of living. Instead of thinking about how to have *more* income, you may benefit far more by thinking about how to have *less* income and building ways to have the same living standard without the tax wedge.

You can read about the many proposals to change Social Security on the Social Security website at https://www.ssa.gov/oact/solvency/index .html. The most important fact is that most proposals die after being studied and talked about.

Chapter 24: The Lifetime Compounding of Un-Money

When money not spent is saved, it can accumulate to a large amount in a working lifetime. You can experiment with different amounts by using a tool provided by our government, https://www.investor.gov/financial-tools-calculators/calculators/compound-interest-calculator.

This is where you learn the long-term cost of luxury spending.

Chapter 25: Health Is All!

Put different assumptions about your personal habits into the John Hancock life expectancy calculator and you'll see how much impact you can have on how long you might live, https://www.johnhancock.com/life-insurance/life-expectancy-calculator.html.

Given the malign neglect of public health, individuals and families will have more impact on their health than government policy will have. That means our active decisions about food and exercise are vital. We also need to avoid the overselling and bad statistics used by long-term care insurance marketers, a reality made very clear by this RAND study, https://www .rand.org/pubs/external_publications/EP67296.html.

Chapter 26: Should You Strive for Early Retirement?

My answer is no – at least for most people. Early retirement is a lovely daydream but it's very difficult for people who have children to raise. The best alternative is to find work you like and find a way to do it, so you want to do it for as long as possible. It can be done. Witness the story of one of my brothers, a former tugboat captain at https://scottburns.com/lets-call-it-reacherism/.

PART VII: MORE COUCH POTATO COOKBOOK – EXACTLY HOW TO DO IT

Chapter 27: The Basic Couch Potato Cookbook

The key to avoiding data confusion is to learn the standardized way primary data sources present their data. For exploring ETFs, www.stockanalysis .com, www.morningstar.com, and www.portfoliovisualizer.com are key sites. All three provide good amounts of data free to nonsubscribers. It's also good to remember that both your 401(k) choices and offers from legacy brokerage firms will view expenses from the perspective of how much they have come down from past levels. They ignore the Couch Potato standard of the lowest possible costs.

Chapter 28: Still More Couch Potato Cookbook

A continuation of Chapter 27, this chapter used the same sources.

ACKNOWLEDGMENTS

E verything we do rests on a foundation of creations and contributions of all those who came before us. This book is no exception. The root of its existence is John Bogle, the founder of Vanguard. He was the prime mover in the creation and development of a mammoth idea: low-cost index investing.

I can't name all the others who have directly contributed to the advancement of that idea, and to my efforts in this book. Charles Ellis saw that professionals were "the market," not individuals. Bill Bengen, Bill Bernstein, Allan S. Roth, and Rick Ferri are essentials. So was Taylor Larimore, the founder of the Bogleheads. Joe Mansueto founded Morningstar, reaching out to retail investors, which counts for a lot. Under its umbrella, Morningstar brought us a long list of fine writers and researchers: John Rekenthaler, Christine Benz, and David Blanchett, for starters.

Beyond that, I've regularly been thankful for Wade Pfau and Michael Finke. They are academics with a concern for actual practices. Like economist Alicia Munnell, who founded the Boston College Center for Retirement Research, they've been vital contributors to the literature of what's possible and how it can be done. My friend, economist Larry Kotlikoff, also bridges deepest academia and public reach. He provided the life cycle framework for this book – and the three books we coauthored earlier.

While Wall Street and the financial services industry fully deserve the beatings included in this book, a handful of people in that industry created the opportunity for low-cost investing. Ned Johnson, at Fidelity, is one. He created one of the first money market mutual funds and enabled small savers to escape the interest rate limits of Regulation Q, the Federal Reserve rule that allowed imposing interest rate ceilings on bank deposits. Later he developed the 401(k) platform that opened the door to lower-cost investing. He also created the first Charitable Gift Fund. Charles Schwab saw the opportunity in deregulation. He drove down the cost of stock transactions. Then he formed the first mutual fund supermarket. State Street Bank and Trust created the first exchange-traded fund in 1993. We can now invest, tax efficiently, for 0.03 percent a year.

Without those creations, we would not have the opportunity to invest at virtually no cost, with no commissions, that we have today.

Bill Falloon, associate publisher at Wiley, is the reason this book exists. He called and said it was time. I don't know how many people he has done this with, but if there is a Library of Index Investing, he built it.

ABOUT
THE AUTHOR

Scott Burns has covered personal finance and economics for over 50 years.

A columnist at the *Boston Herald American* in 1977, he was nationally syndicated in 1981. He joined the *Dallas Morning News* in 1985. His column became one of the most widely read features in the paper, known for reaching all age groups. An easygoing public speaker, he was the most frequently requested speaker at the paper. Prior to his newspaper career, Scott wrote articles and columns for a wide range of magazines, regularly finding humor to make his subject more easily understood.

He has authored or coauthored five previous books. Each examines underexplored aspects of personal and national economics. His first book, *Squeeze It 'Til the Eagle Grins: How to Spend, Save, and Enjoy Your Money* (Doubleday, 1972), was grounded in the life cycle hypothesis.

His second, *Home, Inc.: The Hidden Wealth and Power of the American Household* (Doubleday, 1975), explored the important, but largely ignored, nonmoney economy of families.

He coauthored *The Coming Generational Storm* (MIT Press, 2004) with Boston University economist Laurence J. Kotlikoff. Barron's listed the book as one of the 25 best books of 2004. It warns of a worldwide generational financial crunch.

Their second book, *Spend 'Til the End* (Simon & Schuster, 2008), presents new ideas in financial planning based on consumption smoothing.

Their third book, *The Clash of Generations* (MIT Press, 2012), focused on the collision between entitlement promises and the burden that will fall to our children and grandchildren.

He currently serves as a board and executive committee member for Homeward Bound, Inc., a nonprofit, which is the largest provider of detox and recovery services for the indigent in North Texas.

Scott and his wife live in Texas Hill Country. A fitness fan, he walked the Camino de Santiago, a 480-mile trek in Spain, in 2024.

INDEX